Praise for

WORKING AT WARP SPEED

"This book is too good not to be true. It renews your energy for working and living. For anyone who feels harried, WORKING AT WARP SPEED is an oasis. Stop. Read. Drink."

—Tom Brown, Management General

"A real breakthrough and outstanding introduction to concepts that would otherwise remain hidden in the course of everyday work."

—Colin Clover, manager of technical operations, Apple Computer

"Successful book publishing requires relentless efficiency to manage limited resources, talent, and time. The toughest part is getting everyone on the team on the same page and marching in the same direction. This book shows you how. I wish it had been available thirty years ago."

—Dan Poynter, *The Self-Publishing Manual*

"Everyone who must depend upon others to deliver results by a deadline should read this book. Project management is people management, and here are the rules that make it work."

—Donald M. Dible, cofounder, ProjectWorld

"By sharing the rules of warp speed with a team leader whose team was in full rebellion, I was able to help her quickly grasp the adjustments in her perspective and behavior that made the difference between success and either her dismissal or her team's defection."

—Ira Chaleff, president, Executive Associates

"Barry did an excellent job of putting a fire in me. I can't wait to get back to work and start using these new ideas and techniques."

—Conrad Canderle, SiRF Technology, Inc.

"Over the course of three and one-half years this program has successfully enabled us to blend the demands of those committed to unfettered creative flare and flexibility with those demanding systematic accountability for results. It has helped us maintain momentum, schedules, and—in this incredibly fast paced business—sanity!"

—Jerry Hunt, organization development manager, HAL Computer Systems

"I loved what I read and felt changed by it in a significant way."

—Cindy Flaherty, project manager

"Thanks, Barry! Great class. It should be mandated to all Apple employees so everyone works on the same level."

—Deb Pevarnick-Whitney, Apple Computer

"This is the best-written manuscript I have reviewed. From the very first words, Barry Flicker pulls me in with his concise language, rich insights, and passionate tone. It is a thrill to see such good writing. Over and over again I'd underline an especially insightful thought, then laughed with delight when I turned the page and found it high-lighted."

—Kathleen Epperson, organization effectiveness consultant

"I felt the manuscript was exceptional. Its readability and organization were excellent. My own professional interest is in virtual organizations and I found the problems encountered by the team to be very realistic and the analysis of these problems to be accurate."

—Linda Peters, University of Massachusetts

"Very well done! I can take a LOT out of this. Instructor's knowledge of subject matter is guru status."

"This book is filled with commonsense approaches to improve teamwork and work relationships. I can definitely see using this material in working with clients, or within my own work with nonprofit organizations."

Working at Warp Speed

Working at Warp Speed

The New Rules for Project Success in a Sped-up World

Barry Flicker

BERRETT–KOEHLER PUBLISHERS, INC.
San Francisco

Berrett–Koehler Publishers, Inc.
235 Montgomery Street, Suite 650
San Francisco, CA 94104
Tel: (415) 288–0260   Fax: (415) 362–2512   www.bkconnection.com

ORDERING INFORMATION

Quantity sales. Special discounts are available on quantity purchases by corporations, associations, and others. For details, contact the "Special Sales Department" at the Berrett–Koehler address above.

Individual sales. Berrett–Koehler publications are available through most bookstores. They can also be ordered direct from Berrett–Koehler:
Tel: (800) 929–2929; Fax: (802) 864–7626; www.bkconnection.com

Orders for college textbook/course adoption use. Please contact Berrett–Koehler: Tel: (800) 929–2929; Fax: (802) 864–7626.

Orders by U.S. trade bookstores and wholesalers. Please contact Publishers Group West, 1700 Fourth Street, Berkeley, CA 94710. Tel: (510) 528–1444; Fax (510) 528–3444.

Production Management: Michael Bass & Associates

Printed in the United States of America
Printed on acid–free and recycled paper that is composed of 85% recovered fiber, including 15% post consumer waste.

Library of Congress Cataloging–in–Publication Data

Flicker, Barry, 1949–
    Working at Warp Speed: The new rules for project success in a sped–up world / by Barry Flicker.
        p. cm.
    Includes bibliographical references and index.
    ISBN 1–57675–146–5
    1. Project management. I. Title.

HD69.P75 F56 2001
658.4'02–dc21   2001052437

First Edition

07   06   05   04   03   02   10   9   8   7   6   5   4   3   2   1

To all the generations—

For my grandfather, who taught me unconditional love;

My father, who taught me to trust the universe;

My mother, who taught me to always show up;

My wife, Sharon, who shows me how much happiness
and love is possible;

And all our kids: Blair, Greg, Kier, Clayton, and Jai,
for being so wonderfully who you are.

Contents

Preface

It's like a bad joke. The more labor- and time-saving devices we produce, the faster things go and the busier we get. This is what I've called "working at warp speed." One major drawback to all this hurry is that it encourages machinelike behavior. That is, we rely on the speed of pre-programmed responses to crank out ever more tasks in ever less time. In a sense, that's the punch line of the joke–we seem to be getting nowhere fast. What's worse, something very essential has gotten lost in the process. This book looks at the performance of project teams to discover just how high the cost of this neglect has become, what we can do about it, and why taking action now is so important.

For twelve years, clients have used my Project Master Class to rescue their teams from the depths of despair (or slipping deadlines, whichever came first). The problems they have confronted are predictable, and I have collected them into a kind of "greatest hits" list featuring the ten most common complaints. I use this Warp Speed Barrier Checklist (see page xiii) to begin our work with a simple question.

"Which of these barriers, if any, do you struggle with?"

Invariably the reply is "All of them!" People feel over-loaded, saddled with unrealistic deadlines and constantly expanding scope. They do a poor job defining the goal and planning. Then they become buried in constant firefighting, miscommunication, and conflict while trying to straighten it all out.

I believe you could walk into any company and ask any employee, at random, if they experience any of the barriers on this list and you will likely get the same reply–they struggle with them all.

This universality can surprise people who still think of project management as something reserved for NASA engineers or contractors and high-stakes developers. Most of us have yet to realize how thoroughly project thinking has permeated every aspect of our lives. Have you ever remodeled your home or helped plan a major event like a wedding or fiftieth birthday party? How many times did you have to improvise in the face of an unexpected crisis? That was classic project management. Run a political campaign, make a movie, or organize a group backpacking trip, and you're contributing to a project. In fact, any time you need to get a group of people to complete anything by a deadline you're relying on project fundamentals. Law firms, ad agencies, hospitals, architects, meeting planners, publishers, social activists, you name it–the warp speed barriers confound us all, and we improvise our own version of project management solutions to overcome them.

But why reinvent the wheel when tackling this list of chronic frustrations? Much of the work has already been done, and the results have been collected here, compressed into the pages of this little book. How is that possible? Frantic problems often have simple solutions, as when, after a desperate search, we find our missing glasses perched on the top of our head.

In much the same way, our search for relief from the chaotic pressure of the 24/7 warp speed world results in some obvious but surprising conclusions. The solutions are frequently counterintuitive. The source of the problem is not what we think and often turns up where we least expect to find it. By the end of this book, however, I promise you will discover a set of simple steps that will enable you to find relief from every single one of the Warp Speed Barrier complaints.

Taking you through a simulated training is the easiest way to demonstrate the genesis of this people-centered approach. To this end, I have created a fictional project team. Although the characters are composites, the problems they address are all too real. So, too, are their observations and objections. For instance, the letter from Ellen, in the final chapter, is based on actual correspondence. The behaviors I describe are things that I have watched people re-create day in and day out for over a decade. In other words, I have attempted to make this virtual world as much like the real one as possible.

Some early reviewers suggested that the characters seemed too open to these new ideas and that they should present more resistance. In fact, for the sake of both inter-est and clarity, I have invented far more contention in this simulated classroom than I have ever encountered in the real one. The reason for this lack of resistance, I think, stems from the fact that I do not ask people to take any-thing on faith. We run experiments, observe the results, and, together, draw logical conclusions. Sometimes the results are surprising. If you find any of the outcomes suspect, try running the experiments yourself. I'd love to know what you discover.

For myself, this twelve-year journey of discovery has been a dream come true. I have so many people to thank. At the very beginning, Kelle Olwyler counseled me to become a corporate shaman despite my inability to find that category in the "Help Wanted" section. Tom Pinkson, a real shaman, helped with the inner healing that preceded the outer work. Elaine Hamilton, wherever you are, thanks so much for my first gig. How I got a master consultant like Ron Tilden to mentor me, I'll never know. Ron, none of this would have been possible without you. Dick Miller of Western Learning Systems and Peller Marion kept me working and paying the bills while I learned the ropes. Without my friend and virtual partner, Sue Smith of Effective Training Associates and her incredible staff, I could not possibly be where I am today. To all my extraordinary clients from whom I have learned so much, I can't thank you enough. That goes double for Steve Piersanti and the entire Berrett-Koehler team. Without you, this book would never have happened. In the course of its development, so many extraordinary friends and associates, too numerous to mention individually, gave me the benefit of their insights. Your guidance and encouragement have been indispensable. Most of all, I want to express my love and appreciation to my wife Sharon who kept me going, gave me invaluable feedback through endless rewrites, and has made my life heaven on earth. To all of you, and the Great Mystery from which we have received the miracle of life itself, words are wholly inadequate to express the gratitude I feel.

Barry Flicker
December 15, 2001
Woodacre, California

The Warp Speed
Barrier Checklist

1. Everyone enters the project **running on overload.**

2. Rushing leads to **poorly defined goal**s at the project's inception.

3. **Unrealistic completion date**s leave the team feeling they've been "set up to fail."

4. A sense of urgency encourages **poor communication.**

5. Feeling the crunch, the **planning effort is reduced or skipped** entirely.

6. **Other departments fail to support the project** creating delays.

7. Continued breakdowns trigger **blame and finger–pointing.**

8. **Scope expands** as customers request additional features.

9. **Endless meetings** to sort it all out lack focus, run too long, rehash the same territory, are dominated by a few people, and fail to produce or complete action items.

10. **Constant firefighting** consumes ever more time and effort.

Working at Warp Speed

Introduction
Warp Speed in a Nutshell

Are you working at warp speed–too busy to plan, too rushed to communicate in anything more than e-mail snippets, and too overloaded to read all the e-mail you get? Do overlooked details lead to broken commitments and project problems?

Imagine what your life would be like if you could eliminate the overload; alleviate the struggle to meet "unrealistic" deadlines; reduce the constant firefighting, poor planning, and ineffective communication; and slash the endless time wasted in meetings trying to sort it all out.

It could happen! If only you could get everyone on your team fired up about your project, committed to its success, and pointed in the same direction. But how?

You're about to meet five people who are asking this same question. They need to find an answer–fast. They have overpromised and underdelivered on their projects. Their customers are unhappy, and their time is about to run out. They feel discouraged. At times it seems the harder they try, the worse things get. If they can't turn things around in six months, their next project will be finding work!

Can anything really make a difference? They are skeptical. That is until they see for themselves, through a startling experiment, that they have been solving the wrong problem. Perhaps you have too?

Reading *Working at Warp Speed* could change the way you work forever. It's distilled twelve years of project breakthroughs in leading high-tech companies, top universities, and government institutions into four hands-on rules that can deliver immediate results. These four rules are like the angel in Michelangelo's block of marble–to find them we have only to chip away everything unnecessary. The chipping away takes some time and effort, but the results are well worth it. You will find that they dispel the myth that project management must be boring and highly technical. What's more, they show how anyone can take advantage of this extraordinary system to lighten the workload and ignite the passion of any team.

1

···········

Warp Speed Poisoning

So much to do and so little time—it's the mantra of warp speed. Whenever we depend on others to help us deliver results by a deadline, which is really what projects are all about, the problem grows worse. It can feel like climbing up a wall of sand: the harder we dig in, the more quickly the ground crumbles away beneath us. Working this way can rob us of our joy, undermine a marriage, and destroy our health. Many of us have been working this way for so long it may seem inevitable. It's not. In fact, this way of working is unsustainable. That's why Christi and her team have asked to participate in my Project Master Class. They desperately need some help discovering a way out.

As I prepared the flip charts for our morning session, Christi Qwik whisked into the training room. From her red hair to the New York clip in her delivery, she was a woman who lived and breathed at warp speed, and, in her typical no-nonsense fashion, she wanted to get right down to business. As always she spoke in tones that were crisp and upbeat. But just beneath the surface you could feel the desperation.

"The constantly accelerating pace is killing us," she had told me quite frankly during our first interview.

Christi faced a crisis. As director of information technologies, she needed to "whip her project teams into shape"–fast. Her people maintained the electronic nervous system of the entire organization, but miscommunication and constant firefighting were bringing them closer to nervous breakdown. Work quality had fallen, while repeatedly blown deadlines had become the norm. Key contributors complained about impossible workloads, unrealistic schedules, and unhealthy levels of stress. Customers, both internal and external, were unhappy and growing impatient.

The source of the problem, however, proved slippery to define. During prior interviews, every employee gave a different explanation for what was wrong.

According to Brenda, one of Christi's top project managers, many of the problems began with endlessly shifting objectives demanded by both customers and senior management. Where, in her perpetually overloaded schedule, did they expect her to fit these additional requirements? She did the best she could by pushing herself harder and harder, but this strategy was quickly burning her out. It seemed like the faster she'd go, the slower things went. Somehow she needed more efficient production from her team–especially Al.

Al had a different perspective. He felt Christi created unrealistic deadlines that bore little relationship to the actual work that needed to be accomplished. And Brenda, by accepting these assignments without pushing back more effectively, was setting the team up for failure. He also complained that he rarely had a clear sense of how his task assignments fit into the larger goal. When I asked him if he had shared these concerns with Brenda, he laughed, "She'd never listen."

Dave worked on many of the same projects Al did, but his analysis of the problem couldn't have been more different. Finger pointing only made matters worse, as far as Dave was concerned. The combination of a constantly shifting economy and exploding technological growth seemed to make the current crisis inevitable, leaving little that anyone could really do about it. He just tried to do his job without asking a lot of questions that would only eat into Brenda's already overloaded schedule.

While Dave accepted the status quo, Ellen was angry. As the team's technical superstar, she questioned whether the time had come for her to make a career move. She felt trapped by her success and the endless game of "catch-up." The more she accomplished, the more she was asked to do. Furthermore, she feared that the more dependent the department became on her efforts, the more reluctant they would be to let her move on to new challenges.

Now, as I sat with Christi and her team, I wanted them to see these challenges in a larger context.

"Would it surprise you to know that this same list of frustrations has been driving people in organizations crazy for over fifty years?" I asked them. "Imagine that. Despite all of our spectacular technological advances, your list of frustrations keeps hanging on with the persistence of the common cold. In fact, the faster the technology drives us, the more pronounced the symptoms seem to get. It's a condition I call 'warp speed poisoning,' and I believe that the five of you have named just about every condition on the list."

I then projected a copy of the Warp Speed Barrier Checklist up on the screen so they could see for themselves. I have compiled this list of chronic complaints into a tool I call the Warp Speed Barrier Checklist (see earlier illustration) to lighten the tone a bit. I shared with them my David Letterman–style version called "Top Ten Reasons Why the Job Didn't Get Done":

Top Ten Reasons Why the Job Didn't Get Done

10. Were still in the meeting phase.
Too Many Meetings

9. I'll get to it as soon as I extinguish the flames.
Constant Firefighting

8. I was constrained by the 24–hour–a–day limit.
Scope Keeps Expanding

7. I felt I needed additional criticism.
Blame & Finger–pointing

6. The rest of my team had a golf emergency.
Lack of Support

5. We didn't think it would turn out like this, either. **Poor Planning**

4. I thought, "Are you crazy?" was a health question. **Miscommunication**

3. You wanted it when?!
Unrealistic Deadlines

2. We might have done better if we knew what it was. **Poorly Defined Goals**

And the number one reason why the job didn't get done:

1. The doctor said he's still recovering from the last project. **Overload**

"I'm not sure I get the warp speed part," said Christi. "Like you said, these problems have been around forever. Sure the technology can be a pain in the butt, but it also makes us much more productive. Without it we couldn't compete."

"Right. It's a double-edged sword, isn't it? Going faster leverages our strengths, but it also increases our vulnerability. Think about what happens when you hit a speed bump going sixty miles per hour. At warp speed, minor annoyances become potentially catastrophic disruptions. It has wiped out our margin for error, making us more susceptible to failure and exaggerating the damage when it occurs."

"It sounds like we're trapped," said Dave. "Obviously there's no going back."

"The trap can be sprung if we can identify who's setting the snare and why they're doing it," I told him. "Let's stick with the warp speed barriers for a moment. Who's causing all these problems?"

As they considered this question, I quickly looked through the notes I had taken during my earlier interviews with each of them. I knew, somewhere, they had already provided the answer.

The Idiots Out There

"When we spoke earlier," I said, referring to my notes, "each of you seemed able to identify the culprits. The list included out-of-touch upper management, uncooperative coworkers, and overly demanding customers."

"Don't forget unreliable vendors," Brenda added.

"While you're at it," said Christi, "why don't you include the geniuses in accounting who squeeze our budget and then demand increased functionality?"

BREAKDOWNS

At warp speed,

minor annoyances

become potentially

catastrophic

disruptions.

"That's an impressive list," I said. "It seems like the real cause of all of these problems is the 'idiots out there.' If only these problem people would get their act together, much of our grief would go away. Right?"

Sheepish smiles seemed to indicate we had struck a responsive chord.

"The good news about this explanation," I continued, "is that the problem is somebody else's fault. What's the bad news?"

"We're somebody else's idiot," said Al. That got a laugh.

"We also can't do much about it," Ellen added.

"That's right—other people are not very interested in having us fix them," I agreed.

"Especially if we treat them like idiots," said Dave.

"So how about if we explore the opposite hypothesis—that it's something we're doing, or failing to do, that triggers warp speed poisoning. Of course, the bad news here is that we now own the problem. The good news is, the more squarely we can place ourselves at the root of the problem, the more power we have to change things."

"That's a cute slogan," said Al, "but in practice, I don't buy it. It's not my fault that marketing people make impossible promises to customers with no real sense of what it takes to get a product out the door or that senior management changes priorities every fifteen minutes."

"I agree that it's not your fault, but what if there was some adjustment you could make in your own behavior that could prevent those things from standing in the way of your success? Would you be willing to make that change?" I asked him.

"It depends on what you want me to change," said Al.

"I don't want you to change anything. The real question is, Are you willing to change behaviors that decrease your effectiveness? To help answer that question, we'll run an experiment, and you can assess for yourself in what

RESPONSIBILITY

The more squarely

we can place

ourselves at the root

of the problem,

the more power we have

to change things.

ways, if any, your choices perpetuate the symptoms on the Warp Speed Barrier Checklist. It's a game that will require the five of you to complete a simple project in fifteen minutes."

Al expressed some skepticism about the value of "playing games" while fires burned all around them and wanted to know what "revelation" was going to occur in fifteen minutes that had eluded him during his professional career.

"Given how long you've been at this, Al, I wouldn't be surprised if you've forgotten more about project management than I'll ever know. But obviously something's not working or we wouldn't be having this conversation. If you'll risk fifteen minutes of your time, I can guarantee that you will be shocked at what you discover."

"OK," he conceded reluctantly. "You've got fifteen minutes."

Before moving on, I wanted to make sure that everyone had grasped the major points we had covered. We summarized them as follows:

1. There is a list of ten complaints that have been frustrating people in organizations for fifty years and that we have consolidated into the Warp Speed Barrier Checklist.

2. Most people blame these problems on the "idiots out there," which leaves them innocent but helpless.

3. Therefore, we want to explore the opposite hypothesis—that there is something we are doing or something that we are failing to do that is keeping this list of barriers locked in place.

4. We make this shift in thinking because the more squarely we can place ourselves at the root of the problem, the more quickly and dramatically we can change things.

5. To test this hypothesis, we will run a series of experiments that provide immediate feedback about our real–world predicament.

6. In the past, these barriers may have been tolerated, but, at warp speed, these minor annoyances can become potentially catastrophic disruptions.

We were now going to demonstrate why and how this occurs by playing the Project Game. Only through direct experience can we really appreciate the value of the four rules for project success, and the Project Game would set the stage for our discovering what they are.

2

Playing the Project Game

I knew Al was only half kidding about his fifteen-minute time limit. In the warp speed world, people want everything to be instant except the coffee. So we got right down to business.

"The purpose of this game," I reminded the group, "is to see if we can catch ourselves in the act of creating the very frustrations we identified as standing in the way of our success. Although the game lasts only fifteen minutes, I have attempted to simulate as many real-world conditions as possible.

"For example, take the wide geographical distribution of project coworkers. We will pretend that you must actu-ally coordinate your work over great distances. Therefore, you will not be able to communicate verbally but must use e-mail, which we will simulate by passing handwritten sticky notes."

I then showed them the seating diagram on the next page to explain who could communicate with whom.

Al rolled his eyes. I sensed that he was not thrilled with the pace of the experiment so far.

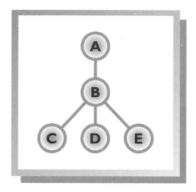

"Once again, to make this as much like actual working conditions as possible," I continued, "I'm going to interrupt your work every five minutes so that we can have a status review meeting."

A number of people, including Al, chuckled ruefully over this line. This was his kind of humor. I explained that, at five-minute intervals, I would ask them to tell me what percent of the project they believed was complete–a practice that mirrored their real-world behavior.

I then asked them each to sit in the chair corresponding with the first letter of their names. In other words, Al sat in chair A, Brenda in B, Christi in C, and so forth. When they were seated, I gave them each an instruction sheet and asked them to begin the first five-minute round.

As they began, a giant quietly slipped into the room. He looked like he could have played center in the NFL and obviously planned on sticking around for a while, so I walked over and introduced myself. That's how I met Tom Costello, Christi's boss. He had dropped by to observe the class. I quickly filled him in on the basics of the game and then tried to give him a feeling for the challenges posed by the exercise.

"The first thing you should know," I told him, "is that team members often begin by assuming the instruction sheets they have been handed are all the same. This is not true. Everyone does receive a set of five different abstract shapes (circles, arrows, squares, and so forth). But only Al, sitting in the A chair, knows that the project goal is to find the one shape all five team members hold in common. The other instruction sheets simply say, 'Here are your symbols.' As a result, Brenda, Christi, Dave, and Ellen will probably spend the fifteen minutes busily passing notes and exchanging information with no idea what they ultimately are trying to accomplish."

"I wouldn't be surprised if some of them find that experience painfully similar to their real jobs," said Tom. "I know a number of folks in Christi's group respond to the enormous time pressure we all work under by resisting all planning efforts. When the consequences of that choice hit them, they act as if they've been tricked and offer a number of different theories as to who it is that's tricked them."

"They're not alone," I told him. "It's difficult for any of us to see the unintended outcomes of our own behavior. Making those outcomes easily visible is exactly what this game was designed to do."

"How does it do that?" Tom wanted to know.

"Well, there's a short answer and a long answer."

"Let's start with the short one," he said.

"Speed forces us to respond automatically," I told him. "Most preprogrammed behavior comes laced with flawed assumptions that generate costly consequences. This game exposes those assumptions so we can make better choices."

"Interesting," he said in a somewhat noncommittal tone of voice. "And the long one?"

"If you'd be willing to wait until the end of the exercise, the discoveries that result would be the most powerful way to provide you with that answer. Forgive me if that leaves you feeling a bit up in the air, but keep in mind that you already have more information about the rules and objectives of this game than any of the players have received. Still, as you try and understand their experiences, you may

CONFUSION

Confusion is

the root cause

of warp

speed poisoning.

feel a sense of confusion," I cautioned him. "Even though you know the goal of the exercise, exactly what people are trying to accomplish may seem unclear. You may wonder who's supposed to be doing what. This is precisely what Christi and her team are asking themselves as they play. This confusion is the root cause of what we've been calling 'warp speed poisoning.'"

"Fair enough. Let's wait and see what happens," Tom said.

At the conclusion of the game, I gave them a few minutes to talk with each other and compare notes. "Look at each others' instruction sheets," I told them. "Find out what was going on and what got in the way."

As they figured out that only Al knew the goal of the exercise, the volume of the conversation rose. Why hadn't he told anyone else? He countered by asking why they failed to follow his simple instructions. When the accusations had subsided, I interrupted their conversation to make the following point.

"I have played this game for over a decade in every conceivable type of organization. I want you to know that there is no mistake you have made that does not occur every time this game is played. These are not personal or organizational failings you have discovered. You have encountered a blind spot in our makeup as human beings."

To help us learn more about this blind spot, I asked if they noticed any parallels between what happened in the game and their experience in real-world projects.

Accelerating in the Wrong Direction

I got the team all fired up but marched them in the wrong direction," Christi said, almost wincing as she spoke.

"And does that ever happen in the real world?" I asked her.

"Are you kidding? Never!" she said with feigned arrogance.

This was met with catcalls and howls of protest from the rest of the group.

"Well, almost never," came her quick revision.

This quieted the angry mob.

"Tell us what happened," I prompted.

She explained that at first she felt confused trying to make sense out of the minimal information on her instruction sheet. As she sat there, inactive and without direction, her confusion quickly morphed into irritation.

"You call these instructions," she said to me, now re-creating the irritation. "Listen to this: 'You may exchange notes only with B'; 'You will find five symbols below'; 'You may not show them to any other person.' There's no goal here."

At the bottom of this page are the symbols:

Christi told us that she immediately dashed off a note to Brenda asking, "What is the goal of this project?" Just as quickly Brenda shot back a reply: "I don't know."

"Now what was I supposed to do?" Christi said, exasperated. "I had no goal, and the only person I could communicate with was as clueless as I was. Meanwhile, valuable time was slipping away and nobody seemed to be taking any action."

"Welcome to my world," said Al.

"Sounds like you were pretty frustrated," I said, addressing Christi.

"We were wasting time, and I felt totally out of control. I hate that feeling."

"So what did you do?"

What she did was redefine the game in a way that enabled her to take control. This also made the uncomfortable feelings go away.

Christi decided that the exercise was intentionally pointless and was meant to test how quickly someone could generate and then mobilize the team around a self-selected goal. Since setting objectives and driving a team to complete them was Christi's strong suit, she could now take decisive action. She immediately dashed off a note to Brenda that read, "Project goal: draw a circle around the square."

With a goal in hand, Brenda got to work sending this information to the other members on the team.

"Al, what did you do when you received that message from Brenda? That must have been confusing given that you already had a different goal on your instruction sheet," I said.

"You asked if there were any parallels with the real world. This is exactly what happens in our projects," Al replied. "I'm told to do one thing and, no sooner do I get started than the priorities change and I'm told to do something else. Here's what my instructions said: 'You are to determine which one symbol is held by all five people on your team.' Then I get this note saying the goal is to draw a circle around the square. What's that about? Are there competing goals in this exercise? Was it a test to see how quickly we could respond to shifting priorities? Who knows? Meanwhile, we're running out of time. If they said the goal was to draw a circle around the square, so be it. I'm just trying to be a team player."

"Let's follow the thread here," I suggested. "The confusing instructions caused you to jump to your own conclusion about the goal of the exercise. This, in turn, confused Al. Confusion and miscommunication continued to cascade throughout the game much as it does in real projects. It's the last thing we intend, yet something drives us toward this counterproductive behavior. Christi, what was it that caused you to jump the gun?"

"I got impatient and, without consulting anyone else, charged ahead with my own ideas about how to get things moving. Since everyone else had an essential piece of information necessary for the completion of the project, that was a big mistake."

"It sounds like taking control, in this instance, came more at the expense of the team," I commented. "Failing to balance control with an appropriate level of team participation gets many projects into trouble. Control has always been a low-quality, brute-force way to get things done. We could get away with this approach as long as we were driving people to complete relatively simple repetitive tasks; for such tasks compliance may be enough. But the warp speed world requires the creative intelligence and flexibility that come from commitment. We can force compliance, but we can only invite commitment."

"This might be a good moment for me to jump in," said Tom. "Unless, of course, I'm disrupting the process."

"Not at all," I told him.

"First, let me apologize to all of you for not being here to kick off the class this morning as I had intended. I got pulled into an emergency meeting the minute I walked in that only just ended.

"That's what I want to talk to you about," he continued. "I know there have been rumors floating around

COMMITMENT

We can force

compliance, but

we can only

invite commitment.

since the beginning of the year as to whether this department will continue. I was just told we've got six months to turn things around and make the case that we are worth more as an independent entity than we cost. If not, we go away.

"So I'm inviting your commitment. As I listened to this discussion, it occurred to me that maybe I've been making the same mistake you did, Christi. I've been trying to muscle things into shape. I've wanted to turn things around by a sheer act of will. Obviously, it hasn't been working. I want to do everything in my power to enable us to succeed, but I can't do it alone. We have a choice. We can either come together and succeed as a team, or we can refuse to change and fail individually."

He paused and looked at them as if searching for that final, inspiring thing to say. I guess the silence was enough.

"Thanks for listening. I'll let you get back to work," is how Tom left it.

The applause that followed had an odd quality. On the one hand, I'm sure people appreciated Tom's candor and integrity. They may have admired his determination to prevail. But there was also a certain awkwardness, like giving the doctor a standing ovation after he announces you only have six months to live.

"It looks like we've upped the ante, but the game is still the same," I told them after Tom had left. "The more effectively we can clear the warp speed barriers, the greater our chance for breakthrough success. And the more squarely we can place ourselves at the root of those problems, the more quickly and dramatically we can change things. So what other parallels did you see between the project game and the real world?"

Confusing Tasks and Goals

"You know, given that we're in a fight for our survival, I think I spend a lot of time doing nonessential activities," said Dave. "At least, that's the way it appears to me. But I don't really know because I'm assigned tasks without context. That's exactly what happened in this game. Nobody ever told me the goal. I went through the entire project without ever knowing what we were trying to accomplish or why."

"Was this true for anyone else?" I asked the group.

"Everyone except Al," said Brenda. "He was the only one who knew the goal, but he didn't tell anybody. And I can't help thinking how ironic that is because not being properly informed is his biggest complaint back at work."

Al immediately took exception to this, insisting that he had, in fact, told Brenda the goal. The two of them began sorting through the pile of sticky notes she had received during the game, trying to find the message that he claimed would vindicate him.

Finally, Al grabbed one of the notes.

"Here it is," he proclaimed, waving the piece of paper about.

"Could you read us what you wrote?" I asked.

"'Collect all symbols from C, D, and E and forward them with your symbols to me.'"

"Is that a goal or a task?" Christi asked him.

Sensing his moment of vindication about to slip from his grasp, Al maintained that this note communicated the goal of the project.

Ellen disagreed. "Finding the one symbol we all had in common was the goal of the project. Having Brenda collect all the symbols and pass them to you was a task designed to accomplish that goal. Your message told her what to do but not why she was doing it."

Al reluctantly conceded the point.

Inclusion—Pros and Cons

In his own defense, however, Al insisted that no one else needed to know the goal for him to complete the objective successfully; in fact, doing so would have wasted too much time. If everyone had followed the first set of instructions he sent to Brenda and passed all their symbols to him, they would have won.

This triggered a heated discussion. Other members of the team explained the confusion and inefficiencies they labored under because they had no idea why they were being asked to do what they were doing. Christi reminded him of the time lost because she tried to guess the objective, thus sending the team on a wild goose chase.

"That's my point," Al fired back. "With all the time we'd already wasted, it didn't make sense to waste more giving everyone a detailed account of the whole project when all you needed to do was follow my simple instructions."

At this point Ellen asked, "What was the goal of this game?"

"To find the common symbol," Al replied.

"Find the common symbol. How long would it have taken to add those four words to the bottom of one of your notes to Brenda—three or four seconds?"

"Maybe, but then she had to make copies to send to everybody else."

"OK. Let's say the whole process would have added thirty seconds–a minute at most. The argument that you didn't have enough time still doesn't hold up when you run the numbers. I think this is typical of what happens in our actual projects. We assume people know things that they don't. Leaving them in the dark slows things down and causes mistakes; this added inefficiency causes us to run short on time, and then we blame the shortage of time for our own failure to communicate."

"It seems that as both Al and Christi became more focused on solving the problem themselves, they stopped asking for or listening to feedback from the team," said Brenda. "Project success requires that we maintain two-way communication at times when doing our own thing would feel much more comfortable."

Al put his hands up in mock surrender. "OK, Brenda, you're right; I'm wrong. You're good; I'm bad. I'm glad we got this all cleared up."

"Come on, Al. This isn't about who's right and who's wrong," said Brenda with a hint of exasperation. "Didn't you hear Tom? Let's not sit here debating whose side of the boat the leak is on. Unless we get it fixed, we're all going down together."

"Brenda, you're right. That's a fair point. I guess it just burns me that I did exactly what frustrates me most about upper management," Al admitted. "I just assumed everybody else had the same information I did. Once I realized they didn't, I still didn't tell them the goal because I thought it would take too much time."

"I think you've just described a catch-22 that we fall into constantly," said Ellen. "We just spent fifteen minutes feverishly passing notes yet were still unable to find the one symbol we all held in common. But once the game

COMMUNICATION

Project success demands

that we maintain

two-way communication

at times when doing our

own thing would feel

much more comfortable.

was over and we sat in a circle sharing information freely, we discovered the common symbol in a matter of seconds. If the actual work solving the puzzle took only seconds, what ate up the rest of the time?"

Everyone agreed poor communication and a failure to coordinate team effort were the obvious answers.

"These communication breakdowns caused us to use our time and resources ineffectively," Ellen continued. "Could poor teamwork and miscommunication also cause our complaints about inadequate time and resources for our projects? I think so."

"I know from my own experience that working in the dark is the biggest time waster of all," said Al. "I can't believe that I did the very thing I most criticize others for doing."

I reassured Al that, after running this game for over a decade, almost everyone who sits in the A chair makes exactly the same mistake and offers the same explanations. That tells me these breakdowns express something very fundamental about who we are as human beings.

Furthermore, I wanted Al to know that when communication breaks down, the team must take responsibility. One person's failure to provide essential information often is mirrored by the failure of others to ask for it.

Why People Don't Ask

When I questioned them as to how many had actually asked for the goal, only Christi raised her hand.

"Brenda, what kept you from asking?" I asked.

She thought for a moment. "I got so overloaded trying to respond to all the notes that I became lost in the detail and forgot."

"Dave, how about you?"

"I don't know. Brenda seemed so overloaded I didn't want to make things more difficult for her. Besides, I figured that if upper management wanted me to know something, they'd tell me."

I have heard some version of Dave's explanation repeated many times over the years. So many of us have learned to be either passive or reactive in the face of authority that creating a proactive, highly committed team takes some work. That work begins by noticing how and why we abdicate opportunities to contribute proactively. In an attempt to explore this idea further, I asked Dave another question.

"It must have gotten boring sitting back there without any idea what was going on. Did you ever try to perk things up by sending any funny notes?"

This question sent both he and Brenda into fits of laughter.

"Well, I was getting kind of hungry sitting back there," he said by way of explaining the laughter, "so I sent Brenda a note asking her, 'What's for lunch?'"

"Did she reply?" I asked.

"That's the funny part," said Brenda. "I quickly dashed off a reply telling him to 'eat his stars,' referring to the symbols on his instruction sheet. But I was writing so fast I accidentally addressed the message to Christi instead of Dave."

"How did that turn out?"

"I had been waiting impatiently for an answer to my second note asking about the goal of the exercise," said Christi "When I received an answer telling me to eat my stars, I concluded that this project was far more complex than I thought."

Christi's deadpan delivery triggered another round of laughter, but there was a certain gallows humor to the joke. They all knew that in their current crisis a little breakdown like this could undermine a project's success and finish them off for good. Perhaps that recognition prompted this observation from Dave.

"I said before that I didn't ask about the goal because I didn't want to increase Brenda's workload, but I'm noticing that somehow I could justify asking her, 'What's for lunch?' That doesn't add up, does it?"

"It sounds like you may also have been committed to something other than team success. Do you have any idea what that might have been?" I asked him.

"It's a little embarrassing to admit, but I think, sometimes, I'm committed to not being blamed for failure. If I don't know something, I can't be held responsible. That way I can be the nice guy, the funny guy, and the helpful guy without becoming the fall guy. I never realized how high a price the whole team was paying for my desire to keep a low profile. It makes me question in what other ways I may be unintentionally sabotaging our success."

Playing this game reveals how small, inconsequential acts that slip by unnoticed during the relentless pressures of everyday work can quickly compound into costly project breakdowns. All of these breakdowns, large or small, share a common denominator that Ellen summarized as follows.

"I see another parallel between this game and the real world," she said. "In each story we've heard so far, Christi, Al, and Dave overemphasized the success of their individual tasks at the expense of the entire system. This happens in our projects all the time. Obviously, if we don't know the goal and don't take time to plan, these types of breakdowns are inevitable."

"It's just like a freeway at rush hour," said Dave. "Metering lights slow down each driver's ability to get on the freeway by a few minutes, but that allows the whole system to keep running more smoothly. Maybe if we did a

SYSTEMS

Overemphasis on the

success of individual

tasks can bog down

the entire system.

better job identifying the bottlenecks in our projects, we could do a better job pacing the flow of work and improve our overall performance."

Unchecked Assumptions

"I like the freeway analogy," said Brenda. "But it brings up another important point. For a system like that to work, everybody needs to be clear what the signals mean and what they are supposed to do in response. That wasn't my experience in the game. For example, I never understood why you refused to tell me your symbols the first time I asked, Dave."

Dave replied: "My instructions said, *'You may exchange notes only with B. You will find five symbols below. You may not show them to any other person.'* I interpreted that to mean that I wasn't supposed to tell you what I had. Then, when I saw everybody else exchanging information, I thought maybe it meant that I couldn't draw the symbols, but I could describe them. Writing all that information out sure took a lot of extra time."

"I just assumed that it meant I couldn't show the instruction sheet to anyone, but it was OK to draw the symbols," Christi added. "It's interesting to see how different interpretations of even one simple sentence can change the outcome of the entire project. Snippets of information exchanged through e-mail can produce similar results. Those little misunderstandings can quickly escalate into finger-pointing and blame—especially when working at warp speed."

Blame, frustration, and boredom can cause us to make further assumptions that undermine team success.

For example, in one session a person sitting in the E chair became so frustrated with the lack of information and feedback that he crumpled up his instruction sheet, threw it on the floor, stormed out of the class, and never came back. He allowed his feelings of indignation to become so overpowering that they shut down his capacity to learn something new.

"If people experience these kinds of feelings in a fifteen-minute game, which ultimately has no real-world conse-quences," I pointed out, "imagine what must be going on in the pressure cooker of a real project environment when financial success and self-esteem hang in the balance."

Emotional static causes us to take our eye off the goal and consumes a great deal of energy. In the lean, just-in-time world of warp speed projects, this reaction is some-thing we just can't afford. Technical tools such as Gantt charts and project software do not address these emotional issues and aren't able to remove these major barriers blocking project success. Project management is people management and must address this emotional component.

"In what way, if any, did emotional static or limiting assumptions alter your commitment to team success?" I asked the group.

"I got buried in detail," said Brenda. "That caused me to start feeling stressed—very much the way I do in my real job. I began to rush and miss important details. It also caused me to focus on answering messages instead of making sense of the entire project."

"I just got bored," said Dave. "Without knowing what we were trying to accomplish or why, the whole exercise just seemed pointless, and I kind of dropped out. That's why I started sending Brenda notes about getting together for lunch."

"You're not alone," I assured him. "I remember one per-son who felt so offended that her time was being wasted that she refused to play. When asked for her symbols, she sent blank notes, and she responded to the questions about percentage complete by saying, 'I don't know and I don't care!'

"She felt very self-righteous about her behavior, insisting that it was an appropriate response to such a stupid game. I asked if she responded this way to real-world situations that she found stupid or ambiguous. She proudly proclaimed that it was–she had no intention of committing to something she didn't care about. Since this attitude doomed her team to failure in the game, I asked her if it had similar repercussions in actual project work. She thought for a moment and then admitted that this was also probably true.

"She acknowledged that she had never looked at it from that perspective before. People who don't care won't commit, and that's a problem because the key to success, in projects as in life, is making and keeping clear commitments."

Everyone agreed that the Project Game had revealed a blind spot in their perceptions about their jobs that caused serious errors in judgment. They concluded that they needed to better understand what was causing this blind spot before they could decide what to do about it.

The Project Game revealed that project management is really people management. The implications of this were expressed in five key insights:

1. Confusion is the root cause of warp speed poisoning.
2. We can force compliance, but we can only invite commitment.
3. People who don't care won't commit. The key to success, in projects as in life, is making and keeping clear commitments.
4. Project success requires that we maintain two-way communication at times when doing our own thing would feel much more comfortable.

5. Overemphasis on individual tasks can bog down the entire system.

All of these observations point to a fundamental blind spot that persistently derails projects. The four rules essential for project breakthrough lie hidden by this blind spot. Before Christi and her team could discover the four keys to project success, this obstruction had to be cleared.

SUCCESS

People who don't care

won't commit.

The key to success,

in projects as in life,

is making and keeping

clear commitments.

3

Seeing the Blind Spot

You glance in both the driver's side and rearview mirrors and see a clear lane to your left. You put on your turn signal and begin changing lanes. Suddenly, there's the bone–chilling blare of a car horn. You veer to the right, narrowly avoiding a collision. With your heart pounding, you make vivid hand gestures of apology as the driver in the other car shoots you a dirty look. Still caught in an adrenaline rush fueled by feelings of embarrassment and relief, you admonish yourself always to look over your left shoulder before changing lanes. Because you know about the blind spot, you recognize that it was your own actions that precipitated this brush with death. You also know that, to avoid future incidents, it is you who must take corrective action.

But what if you didn't know about the blind spot? You might find your fear turning into rage. This other driver almost killed you. The lane was clear in both mirrors before you signaled. Why doesn't he watch where he's going? The idiot was probably talking on his cell phone. This time, as he drives by shooting you his dirty look, you probably make very different hand gestures. Very little useful learning will result from this perspective, and the odds are quite high that you will find yourself in this situation again.

Before playing the Project Game, this is very much like the predicament Christi and her team found themselves in. Their own counterproductive behavior was hidden in a perceptual blind spot that caused them to repeat it again and again. The worse things had gotten, the more bitterly they blamed the idiots out there until they found themselves in a do–or–die situation.

Did the Project Game make this clear to them? Could they now recognize what was causing the blind spot and identify the behaviors undermining their success? These were the questions with which we began our next inquiry.

"What caused the blind spot in the Project Game?" I asked them.

"The lack of communication," said Al.

"How about our tendency to try and force things to happen through control and compliance rather than building commitment?" Brenda added.

"Anything else that you want to add to that list?" I asked them.

"I liked the points Ellen and Dave were making about projects functioning like systems," Christi said. "Overemphasizing individual tasks can bog down the entire system."

"These are all important points," I said. "Often, when we think about projects, we focus on tasks and deadlines, but communication, commitment, and systems focus on something else. There's something that ties them all together. Any thoughts about what that might be?"

Eventually Brenda broke the silence with a single word that came out sounding more like a question than a statement.

"Relationships?"

"In what way?" I asked her.

"Commitments define our relationships by setting clear expectations. Effective communication sustains our relationships by confirming that our commitments were met. And a systems perspective harmonizes the relationships within a project and keeps them from working at cross purposes."

"Neglected relationships represent a huge blind spot in the warp speed world," I agreed. "The Project Game shows us specific ways in which those relationships break down."

To better understand what the Project Game might have been showing us about these relationships, we began by identifying who, in the real world, filled each of those roles. They quickly agreed that B represented the project manager and that C, D, and E were the individual contributors that made up the core team. Identifying A was a little less clear. Brenda said it was Christi, while Christi said it was Tom. Others suggested that it could be marketing. They all agreed that the function of that role was to hand off the project to the project manager and provide him or her with a clear picture of the goal from the customer's perspective. For this reason we decided to call the person in the A chair the "customer contact." We concluded that communicating across different layers of the organization could lead to breakdowns when satisfying individual task requirements caused us to neglect integrating these layers.

To help us visualize this more clearly, I showed them the following map.

"The Project System map enables us to look at all the players, see how they are connected, and consider what kinds of commitments they need to make to each other. For example, what kind of commitment does the customer contact need to make to the customer?"

"That he will deliver the solution that the customer wants," said Ellen.

THE PROJECT SYSTEM

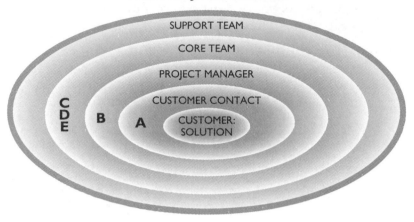

"In the real world, why does that commitment break down?" I asked.

"Failing to ask enough questions or the right questions can result in a poorly defined goal," said Christi.

"Failing to stay in close enough contact with the customer as things change can also produce an unacceptable solution," Ellen added.

"How about failing to communicate the goal to the project manager?" said Brenda. "When the person in the A chair tries to save time by only communicating tasks, all kinds of mistakes start to happen."

"That's an important point to keep in mind," I said, amplifying Brenda's observation. "The customer contact has important commitments to the project manager as well as the customer. This is true at every level. Just as A must keep the interests of the customer and project manager harmonized, the project manager must perform that same function for the core team and the customer contact. In larger projects, where each core team member may lead a small support team, each core team member must keep communication flowing between their subteam and the project manager.

"Under the pressure we feel to complete specific tasks, we often lose sight of the necessity to balance what may be conflicting needs of the different layers that depend on us," said Brenda.

"Performing tasks tends to be easier than sorting out relationships," I added. "While tangible outputs are perceived as central to project success, communication may seem like excess baggage that, for the sake of efficiency, should be kept to a bare minimum. While tasks can be quantified and clearly defined, relationships and communication are apt to be messy, and even uncomfortable. We tend to overemphasize what we can measure and avoid what we can't. Until we learn how to deal with this blind spot, we will keep causing collisions. Poorly managed relationships are the project blind spot. Does this make sense?"

Their heads were nodding yes, but were they committed or just complying? Could they now see what it would take to turn things around? That was the real test, and it was time to find out.

RELATIONSHIPS

Poorly managed

relationships

are the project

blind spot.

4

The Rules of Warp Speed

Given the pattern of breakdowns you've observed playing this game, can you identify any rules that will enable you to run your projects more effectively?" I asked the team.

"Always communicate the goal to the entire project team," Al offered.

"That's good, but I'm not sure it goes deep enough." Brenda added. "One of the things this exercise underscored for me is the huge gap between what we know and what we actually do. Always communicating the goal is the perfect example. As you pointed out earlier, Al, that's one of your biggest frustrations back on the job, and I think you see me as the main source of that problem. But the minute you sat in the A chair you failed to act on what you already knew."

"I think you're onto something," said Christi. "We all fell into the trap of knowing one thing but doing something far less effective under pressure. I think we're missing something in ourselves that stands between the knowing and the doing."

"You mean a blind spot," said Al.

"Well, we've sure caused more than our share of collisions," she replied.

Upon closer examination, failure to communicate the project goal seemed to be a single component of a much broader communication breakdown. They decided to list the other instances of miscommunication and see if they could find a fundamental misstep that tied them all together. The list included Christi's sending the team on a wild goose chase with a false goal, Al's confusion of task and goal, and Dave's counterproductive participation choices.

Ellen pointed out that, in each case, people had acted on unchecked assumptions. For example, while Christi assumed that no one knew the goal and therefore she needed to invent one, Al assumed that everyone knew the goal or didn't need to know. Dave cut himself out of the loop by assuming that if he were supposed to know something somebody would tell him.

"I think what we're saying is, Don't make assumptions," said Al.

"In a warp speed world, assumptions are inevitable," said Dave. "I think it was our failure to check those assumptions that created the unnecessary confusion and wasted so much time. If we had done a better job of including each other, we could have eliminated that lack of clarity. That's exactly what happened when we all sat in a circle."

"How about 'Avoid confusion through inclusion'?" Al suggested.

"Inclusion reminds us to keep communication flowing between layers," said Ellen, "and I think the rhyme is cute."

"Let's write it down," said Brenda.

So Ellen wrote down on the whiteboard:

THE RULES OF WARP SPEED

- AVOID CONFUSION THROUGH INCLUSION.

"That's a good starting point," said Christi, "but it raises another concern. Al, you and I have had a number of conversations about senior management not keeping you better informed. It seems to me that 'Avoid confusion through inclusion' is a principle that you've championed strongly long before this class."

"That's right," he said, as if someone had just challenged him to step outside.

"Don't get me wrong," said Christi, picking up on the edge in his voice, "I agree with you. I'm just noticing how easy it is to believe one thing and to do something quite different under pressure. After all, when you sat in the A chair you fell into the same trap I do. I think we need to ask ourselves why this somewhat obvious rule is so easily and consistently violated."

Again, reviewing their experience in the Project Game, everyone agreed they felt rushed. By acting too quickly some people were left out, mistakes were made, and key pieces of information were overlooked that caused everything to take more time.

"How about 'Go slow to go fast'?" said Brenda.

"That's part of the answer," Christi agreed, "but we don't want to always go slow. Sometimes we need to go fast to go fast. I think what we may be noticing is that we need to pace ourselves. Taking more time in the beginning stages may enable us to spend a lot less time overall."

"I've got it!" said Al. "'Shift from racing to pacing.'"

"I like that," said Ellen, "and I think it further explains why overemphasis on individual tasks can produce a net loss for the entire system."

"Help us make that connection," I asked her.

"If any one layer of the project system moves so quickly that a dependent layer can't keep up, communication between them will break down. That could ripple through the entire system. For example, when Brenda

rushed to clear her growing pile of messages, she accidentally sent Christi the note that said 'Eat your stars.' From
Brenda's perspective the quicker she wrote, the more messages she cleared off her desk. She didn't know, until after
the game, that her increased productivity came at the
expense of the entire team."

"Now I feel guilty," said Brenda.

"Wasn't it you who said, 'It doesn't matter whose side of
the boat the leak is on'?" said Al.

"Thanks for the reminder," said Brenda. "If we could all
just remember to do what we already know, we could
probably improve our performance 100 percent."

"That's what these basic rules are intended to do," I told
her. "They create a simple, easily remembered shorthand
that keeps us focused on core success factors. That's why I
like Al's rhyming scheme. It's easy to remember."

While we were talking, Ellen had added Al's second
contribution to the list as follows:

THE RULES OF WARP SPEED
- AVOID CONFUSION THROUGH INCLUSION.
- SHIFT FROM RACING TO PACING.

Continuing this line of inquiry, the obvious follow-up
question was "What's causing us to rush?"

"The pace of technological change," said Christi.

"Constantly shifting priorities," said Brenda.

"A bunch of clueless marketers that promise customers
the moon without ever checking with us to find out what's
really possible," said Al.

"Let me break in for just a moment," I requested. "I
understand that these are all legitimate frustrations that
you deal with constantly. But notice that these explanations all blame the 'idiots out there,' which leaves you with
very little power to change things. Keep in mind that rushing caused the same kind of breakdowns in the Project

Game that you describe frustrating you in the warp speed world. However, in the Project Game, none of these external factors were present. Strip away technological change, shifting priorities, and clueless marketers, and something else still pushed you into overdrive. What was it?"

At first this question generated a vast and prolonged silence. Getting past conventional wisdom takes patience. We waited.

"I grew impatient," said Christi.

"Overload makes me a little frantic," Brenda admitted.

"When I get frustrated, I sometimes make snap decisions," said Al. "I try to take shortcuts that can lead to dead ends. The backtracking wastes more time, increases my frustration, and causes me to rush even more."

"For me, it begins with an uncomfortable feeling in the pit of my stomach," said Dave. "I guess it's fear or anxiety. Whatever, I just want it to go away and I rush to get it over with. I guess sometimes what I call rushing is actually seeing a problem and then running for safety."

"I think I do something similar, only the trigger for me is boredom," said Ellen.

"There's a guy by the name of Mihaly Czikszentmihalyi . . . ."

"Could you spell that?" asked Al.

"Yes, just not correctly," I said, trying to meet fire with fire. "But it's pronounced 'chick–sent–me–high' in case you ever want to repeat what I'm about to tell you. Anyway, he's a psychologist at the University of Chicago who has studied peak performers in business, the arts, and athletics for over twenty years. He has identified a state of effortless excellence that he has called a 'flow' state and that many athletes describe as 'the zone.'

"When we experience a task as too easy, we feel bored; too difficult and we feel anxious and overwhelmed. In between boredom and anxiety we have access to this zone of effortless excellence—an integrated state of unlimited possibility."

A light seemed to be going on for Christi. "So, from this perspective, we want to push ourselves and each other to the point that we feel excited by the challenge but not so far that we throw up our hands in defeat."

"Exactly. It's that excitement that generates caring and commitment, and it's the frustration and overwhelm that shuts it down."

"Then it would seem that the third law would be something like 'Work from the zone,'" said Dave. "Earlier we said 'People who don't care won't commit.' Working from the zone seems like a prerequisite to commitment."

The team liked Dave's suggestion, and Ellen rearranged the bullets on the whiteboard accordingly. When she was done it looked like this:

THE RULES OF WARP SPEED
- WORK FROM THE ZONE.
- SHIFT FROM RACING TO PACING.
- AVOID CONFUSION THROUGH INCLUSION.

Just to make sure that everyone was on the same page with this rapidly developing logic train, I asked Ellen to clarify why she had rearranged the order of the statements.

"Well, we noticed that most of our mistakes seemed to stem from a lack of inclusion. In asking why we left people out of the loop, we decided that we were moving too quickly and needed to pace ourselves. Finally, when we considered what was pushing us into overdrive, you pointed out that feelings of anxiety, fear, or boredom could push people out of the zone—causing them to use both their own and other people's energy inefficiently. Since urgency leads to rushing, the sequence seemed to be zone, pacing, inclusion."

"Great, I got it. Do those three cover all the bases?"

"I think we need to say something about our definition of success. So far, we've described what makes for a successful journey, but we still haven't identified our destination," said Christi.

"I think that's pretty self-evident," said Al. "Our goal is to deliver a product that meets specification, time, and budget requirements."

"Suppose, after achieving that goal, you send a note to all the team members congratulating them on a job well done and nobody knows what to feel good about because they were never told the goal?" Dave countered.

"Granted that's a mistake, but our goal is satisfying the customer, not each other."

"Satisfying the customer is an essential measure, but not the only one," Ellen added. "We could satisfy customers by selling product at or below cost, but that would soon put us out of business. Continually frustrating our key employees could produce much the same result."

"Or burning them out!" Brenda added. "Running on reserve is an emergency procedure, not a way of life. At least not the way I want to live my life. The way I've been living lately is insane. I shouldn't even say 'living'–all I do is work. I know one thing: that's got to change–and fast!"

"I agree," said Christi. "Both the project and the people must be fulfilled."

"That sounds like the fourth rule to me," said Ellen, and since no one objected, she added it to the list.

Translating the final list onto a finished overhead produced a chart that looked like the one on page 50:

These rules seem pretty obvious once people have played the Project Game and begin to notice how they have limited their own success. But are these the things most people think of when they first hear the words project management? Not likely. When asked about their own

THE RULES OF WARP SPEED

• **Work from the Zone**

• **Shift from racing to pacing**

• **Avoid confusion through inclusion**

• **Both the project and the people must be fulfilled**

associations during our interviews, Christi's team said things like "unrealistic schedules," "too many meetings," "MS Project," "Gantt charts," "work breakdown structure," and "critical path." In other words, their thinking focused on problems and technical tools. By formulating these new rules, they had signaled a radical shift in their perspective, and I wanted to make sure that they were aware of that.

When I say that project management is really about people management, people smile and nod their heads in agreement. Who wouldn't? It's kind of like saying you're for Mom and apple pie. But when we look at what people actually do–in real projects and in the Project Game–a very different set of values emerge.

When people push themselves and others harder than they want to be pushed to get things done faster, schedules become techniques for applying pressure. Coworkers become a means to an end; once we have what we need from them we can move on. In this context, people management means control, and control is all about power. The chronic frustrations outlined in the Warp Speed Barrier Checklist are the inevitable outcome. I summarized our discussion about project relationships as follows.

"The new rules you have proposed define a different reality–a reality based on reciprocal rather than power relationships. The advantage of reciprocal relationships became obvious the minute you pulled your chairs into a circle and noticed that you worked much more quickly and efficiently.

"These four rules give you a simple way to test whether you're playing the reciprocal game or the power game. If you find that you've slipped back into the familiar power game, they show you how to shift gears into reciprocal relationship. That shift will begin to resolve every issue on the Warp Speed Barrier Checklist."

"That's quite a sweeping statement," said Al.

"You don't have to take my word for it," I told him. "Go out there, apply the rules, and see for yourself."

"I'm willing to do that," said Brenda. "But how do we overcome the resistance from people who haven't been through this class?"

"What kind of resistance are you imagining?" I asked her.

"Boy, you name it. People who feel like sitting in a circle communicating is a waste of time. People upstream who don't think it's important for us to know the goal or assume we already know it."

"Or how about people like the woman you described who refused to play the game because she thought it was stupid?" asked Ellen. "How do you motivate people to play by a new set of rules when they think the game itself is stupid?"

"It sounds like we're ready to take a look at how to implement these new rules. Let's start right here, right now. Notice how you feel when you think about all the resistance that you're going to meet. Are you in or out of the zone? We don't need other people to knock us out of the zone. Our own fear takes care of that quite nicely. With only six months left to live, we don't have time for that. We've got to find out what turns you and your team on immediately and start working from there. That's what it means to work from the zone."

RESOLUTION

Shift from power

to reciprocal relationships

and you can resolve

every issue on the

Warp Speed

Barrier Checklist.

5

Work from the Zone

Since you're concerned about meeting resistance, let's start by considering how we might gain the buy-in of others," I said as I threw several scraps of paper on the floor. "For example, who wants to volunteer to clean up these scraps of paper?"

Nobody volunteered.

"Come on, Al. How about you?"

"Sorry, it's not in my job description."

"Ellen, can you help out?"

"How soon do you need it done?" she wanted to know.

"Right away."

"That's not possible. I've got half a dozen priority assignments that are already running late."

"Somebody, please. Dave, what about you?"

"I've never really done that kind of work before," he whined, to the delight of the group. "I really think you should give such an important assignment to somebody more experienced. How about Brenda?"

"Don't you be looking at me," said Brenda, "unless you're going to tell me how to deal with all those excuses. What you just went through is what I face every single day."

"Let's run the experiment one more time," I suggested.

This time I grabbed a wad of bills from my pocket and tossed them into the air so that they fluttered to the floor. Amid the laughter, Christi pretended to lunge out of her seat eager to help me clean up the scattered twenty-dollar bills.

"See–no more excuses; now everybody wants to pitch in and help. Why?"

"There's an obvious payoff," said Ellen.

"Exactly. No convincing or arm twisting is required when the value of work is obvious. It happens automatically."

"We don't usually have the ability to offer cash bonuses at our level of the organization," said Al.

"I use money because it makes for a quick, powerful demonstration. But that's not what's getting most people out of bed in the morning," I replied. "People act on what they care about. If you want to motivate someone, you must understand what it is they value. If you can forge an unmistakable link between what they care about and what you want them to do, they will be lunging out of their chairs to help."

"So instead of just asking people to complete a task, we could take the time to learn how our project could give them a chance to contribute and then build on that enthusiasm," said Ellen.

"I like that approach," said Christi. "You could point out how participating in your project might present them with the opportunity to sharpen a particular skill set, work with certain people they'd like to get to know, or learn about a new aspect of the technology."

"Those are noble sentiments," said Ellen. "The question I want answered is, Are we going to do anything about them? I've wanted to sharpen my skill set and work with

MOTIVATION

If you can forge an

unmistakable link

between your wants and

their values, they'll

be lunging out of

their chairs to help.

some new people for months, but it sure hasn't worked out that way. Does this mean that you'll finally help me get that transfer?" she asked Christi.

The sudden intensity of Ellen's remarks silenced the room so completely we could hear a distant lawn mower manicuring the grass somewhere on the campus. Finally, Christi spoke.

"Look, Ellen, I'm sorry you're frustrated—I really am. I know you want to transfer to another department and I'm doing the best I can to accommodate you, but so far the opportunity hasn't presented itself. Meanwhile, I have projects to run. I depend on the work you're doing now to make that happen."

"Ellen, let's do a quick check-in. Right now are you in or out of the zone?" I asked her.

"Definitely out."

"It sounds like you feel trapped."

"I feel like I've tried everything," she said, as if pleading her case.

"Feeling stuck or trapped triggers our fight-or-flight programming. Fight-or-flight knocks us out of the zone; overriding it opens the doorway back in. Here's the trick. Suppose you knew, for a fact, that over the next few months, this situation would resolve itself in your best interest. Would you still feel angry and defensive?"

"Well, of course not, but I still wish I'd been treated better."

"That still sounds angry and defensive. Defensiveness makes us react to our own fear instead of the full range of options available. That's why it tends to be counterproductive. Here's the deal: Would you be willing to totally let go of anger and defensiveness in return for a positive outcome to your problem?"

"Obviously I want to say yes, but it's not so easy to do."

"Is there anyone here who hasn't faced a similar challenge at sometime?" I asked the group.

Not only could everyone relate to Ellen's predicament, but they were also very interested to see how it was going to resolve.

"When we're trying to move from fight–or–flight back into the zone, there are three things it is helpful to keep in mind," I suggested. "First, fight–or–flight feeds on feelings of isolation. The fact is, we're in this together. As Brenda pointed out earlier, it doesn't matter whose side of the boat the leak is on. If it sinks, we all go down.

"Second, fight–or–flight convinces us that we're trapped in a life–and–death struggle. The fact is, there is always a way through. Our fear keeps us from seeing it by presenting a very limited and distorted picture of the situation. For that reason, the third thing you need to do is see where you really are."

"I'm with you in theory," said Ellen, "but practically speaking, how does any of this help my situation?"

"Why wouldn't anyone help pick up the paper in the first experiment?" I asked her.

"They didn't see anything in it for them."

"Exactly. The instant people see a payoff they no longer need convincing. So what's the payoff for Christi to send one of her most effective employees off to another department?"

"I see what you mean," she said. "The way I set things up created a classic win/lose scenario. If I get what I want, Christi loses. If Christi gets what she wants, I lose. If I could define my next challenge in terms that would solve a problem for Christi rather than create one, she'd probably be more motivated to help me."

"Now you see where you really are," I added. "You're in a system with Christi and others. Once we accept that

ZONE GUIDELINES

- We're in this together.

- There's always a way through.

- See where you really are.

we're in this together, we can begin to craft creative solutions that harness the forces that previously seemed to stand in our way. When we follow the current instead of resisting it, there's always a way through."

"I have to take some responsibility for this situation as well," said Christi. "First, I want to apologize, Ellen. I've been telling myself that I've been doing all I can to act on your request, but I see now that, to some degree, I have been avoiding it because I didn't want to lose you. If you're not happy, I'm going to lose you anyway. I have some ideas that I'd like to talk to you about later. But if those don't suit you, I will make sure that we get you into a situation that will provide you with the challenges and rewards you deserve–even if that means losing you to another department."

"Thanks. It feels really good to hear you say that," said Ellen.

"I can't tell you how relieved I feel to hear you both talking this way," said Brenda. "We may all be in this together, but I've felt like I've been caught in the middle. I have been very upset over this situation." She put her hand to her chest and began to laugh. "Oh, my gosh. I don't think I realized how really bothered I was until just now."

Warp speed urgency convinces us that we can't afford to waste time sorting out messy conflicts. When we sweep these issues under the rug, they can take the whole team out of the zone, not just the people directly involved.

"Well, maybe we could put this approach to another real–world test," said Christi.

"What did you have in mind?" I asked.

"Like Ellen, I also have a point of ongoing frustration with my boss–scope creep."

"By 'scope creep,' you mean the addition of features and requirements without providing additional time or resources?" I asked her.

"Exactly," Christi replied. "If I say yes to an unreason-able request and then fail to deliver, I get blamed. If I say no, I sound uncooperative and it can easily become a power struggle. I'm sure I don't need to spell out who gets the short end of the stick in a power struggle with my boss."

"Yeah, and let's not forget that 'stuff' rolls downhill," Al quickly interjected. "What you promise gets passed on to Brenda to deliver, but it's us worker bees that get stuck grinding out the impossible workload."

Ellen and Dave both nodded in agreement.

"I noticed you referred to these encounters as a power struggle," I commented. "The minute we see ourselves in a win/lose struggle, the fact that we're in this together gets lost as well. Are you and Tom in this together?" I asked Christi.

"We better be or we're history."

"Then let's take a look at where you really are, starting with the story you tell yourself that makes this look like a power struggle."

"When difficulties arise around expanding scope, there's a good chance Tom has been pressured by some-body else," she replied. "I think sometimes he just wants to get the problem off his desk and dumps it on me."

"Illegal dumping is always nasty business. What do you feel he should have done instead?" I asked.

"He should have taken a more active role in resolving the issue himself."

"What's the common theme in both Ellen's and Christi's conflicts?" I asked the group.

"They both felt mistreated," said Dave.

"Isn't that what generally knocks us out of the zone— how unfairly my husband or wife treated me, or my par-ents, or my best friend, or my boss? But now we know that there's always a way through, so what can we do about it?"

"Get even," said Al.

"That's right, or we can go away. Those are the options our fight–or–flight thinking offers us. Where does that leave us?" I asked the group.

"It leaves us angry, frustrated, and at the mercy of the idiots out there," said Ellen.

"Any suggestion that could help Christi shift her power struggle into a reciprocal relationship with Tom?" I asked.

Brenda had a suggestion. "We saw, in the Project Game, that things that look impossible may turn out to be more doable than we thought. Maybe the things that Tom asks us for are more doable than we think. Instead of immediately reacting we could suspend judgment until we've had a chance to run the numbers."

"Good. We can avoid reacting prematurely. Any other ideas?"

"Plug the additional tasks into our project plan and take a look at the impact," said Al.

"OK, and then . . . ?"

"Review the results with the team at the next status meeting, and see if we can find a way to rework the plan to accommodate the change," he continued.

"And if not?"

"Come up with three options that Christi can take back to Tom," suggested Ellen.

"Thanks, everyone," said Christi. "These are great suggestions, and I know that if I took the time to go through these steps, Tom would be very responsive. With the right information and a positive attitude, we would find a way to work through these scope changes to provide a better outcome for the customer while causing less wear and tear on all of us. Unfortunately, I get so sped up I forget to do what I already know."

"That's why proper pacing is so critical. We're in this together, but it won't feel that way if I move so fast that I run right by you. There's always a way through, but if, in my hurry, I spend all my energy paddling against the current, it's going to be a long and painful journey. If we're going to see where we really are, we better take a moment to slow down."

"Who has time for any of that?" asked Al.

Although I knew he was more or less kidding, Al's comment reminded me to slow down myself and review the essential ideas we had covered.

1. Zone Guidelines include "We're in this together," "There is always a way through," and "See where you really are."

2. If you want to motivate people, forge an unmistakable link between your wants and their values, and they will be lunging out of their chairs to help.

3. Warp speed urgency convinces us that we can't afford to waste time sorting out messy conflicts. When we sweep these issues under the rug they can take the whole team out of the zone, not just the people directly involved.

4. Defensiveness makes us react to our own fear instead of the full range of options available. That's why it tends to be counterproductive.

5. With the right information and a positive attitude, we can find a way to work through scope changes that provide a better outcome for the customer while causing less wear and tear for the team.

Working from the zone calls attention to how we are feeling. Some people operate under the misconception that having or expressing feelings at work is, in and of itself, unprofessional. Feelings are not a biological mistake. They are an essential part of our ability to work together and succeed. How we feel impacts how we think and behave.

Our behavior, in turn, influences how we feel. For example, when we become overloaded, we feel stress and anxiety, which eventually lowers our performance and efficiency. That's why effective pacing is so important. Working from the zone and proper pacing go hand in glove, which is why it was the focus of our next inquiry.

6

Shift from Racing to Pacing

Just like it takes money to make money, it also takes time to make time. Common sense tells us that we must learn to walk before we can run. But the urgency of warp speed consistently overrides this common sense. Consequently, we speed up when we need to slow down, and we confuse activity with effectiveness. Doing the wrong thing faster and faster only accelerates our failure rate.

The mechanism that keeps this counterproductive behavior locked in place is captured perfectly by a Zen parable.

A professor of philosophy has become fed up hearing his students singing the praises of an old Zen master. Determined to get to the bottom of all the mystical mumbo-jumbo, he goes to the monastery to find out what this Zen thing is all about. The master tells the professor that he will gladly share his teachings, but first they must have tea. Irritated, the professor insists that he is much too busy for such niceties. The master is equally clear—no tea, no Zen.

Reluctantly the professor agrees to have tea. The Zen master seems very happy. He slowly unwraps a paper parcel and pours leaves into a mortar and pestle. He grinds the leaves and places them in a bamboo strainer. Lighting a small charcoal brazier, he places water on to boil. While waiting for the water, the Zen master begins arranging flowers. The ever more irritated professor keeps looking at his watch.

Eventually the tea is ready. The Zen master hands the professor a cup and begins to pour. He slowly fills the cup halfway, three quarters, to the brim and continues to pour until it is spilling onto the floor.

"What's the matter with you?" screams the professor, as he pulls away the overflowing cup. "Can't you see it's full and that no more will go in?"

"First lesson in Zen," says the master. "Nothing more can be added to an already full cup. You came here to learn about Zen, but you were full of your own opinions. Before we can learn anything new, first we must empty the cup."

The warp speed world keeps filling our cups with an endless stream of accelerating data, deadlines, and demands. This creates the illusion that we are in a constant state of learning and innovation. But if the outer world keeps changing while we keep responding with our same old behavior patterns, we are actually growing increasingly out of touch.

This is the problem faced by Christi and her team. They find their cups kept so constantly full that they are unable to pace themselves appropriately, open to new possibilities, or create a brighter future. Is it possible to slow down, even for a moment, when working at warp speed? This is the question with which we began our next inquiry.

"Christi, when we first spoke, you told me that the constantly accelerating pace was killing you. What's making you run so fast?"

"We either grow faster than we can hire, or we down-size faster than the workload shrinks," she said.

"The volume and pace of our projects too often are dictated by our competition or sudden shifts in the market," Ellen added.

"Another factor is that marketing makes promises to customers that bear little relationship to our capacity to actually deliver," said Dave.

"In each of these examples, who's setting your agenda?" I asked them.

"The idiots out there," said Al.

"Do you remember what happened, in the Project Game, when Brenda let the volume of messages define how she played?" I asked.

Brenda was quick to respond.

"I tried working so fast that I misread information, sent notes to the wrong people, and overlooked key communications."

"You can never empty a cup that other people constantly refill."

"But I have a hard time saying no to people," she said.

"Why?" I asked her.

"I guess I don't want to disappoint them."

"But isn't that exactly what you do when you make commitments that you can't fulfill?"

She agreed that that was true.

"It may look like it's other people who are causing you to run on overload, but it's not. You own your agenda."

"It sure doesn't feel that way most of the time," she said.

"Let's try an experiment to see why that is," I suggested.

I explained to them that we were going to attempt to manage a very simple agenda. We were going to attempt to keep our attention focused on our breathing for one minute.

Emptying Your Cup

"Just notice the air moving in and out of your body for sixty seconds," I instructed. "If you find that thoughts about work or personal concerns interrupt your focus, simply return your attention to your breath. At the end of one minute, you will again hear the chime sound. At that time, please open your eyes and let's talk about your experience."

"Do we have to chant 'Om'?" asked Al.

"If that's what you'd like, Al, that's fine." I said.

Sixty seconds equals about ten breaths in and out. When we were done, I asked them what they had noticed.

"It was great," said Brenda. "I almost fell asleep it was so restful. I wanted to keep going."

"I was amazed at how hard it was to stop thinking about work even for sixty seconds. I'd try and pay attention to my breathing and the next thing I know I'd be reviewing my e-mail or mentally preparing for my next meeting," Christi added.

"That's what's running our agenda most of the time—preprogrammed responses that worked in the past. Isn't it amazing to see how difficult it is to turn them off?" I asked her.

"It's almost embarrassing," she said. "I consider myself a very disciplined person. Seeing that I couldn't keep my mind focused on one thing for sixty seconds is very disturbing."

"It's a problem we all face," I told her. "The problem gets compounded in a world of warp speed change. Do past successes still make sense in the changed environment? We need to slow down long enough to find out."

"I can see how taking a minute to clear my mental space in the midst of the daily insanity could help me make better decisions and function at a higher level of efficiency," said Ellen. "It was like taking a ten-breath vacation."

"A ten-breath vacation," Dave repeated, "I like that. Another benefit I experienced was noticing more of what was going on around me–like the sound of air conditioning turning on or people's conversations in the hallway. At first, I thought about this as a distraction and it made me frustrated. Then I noticed that everything had a certain rhythm or cycle to it. At that point they stopped becoming distractions and began blending with my breathing."

"When we slow down long enough to notice the relationship between things, we can often see how to use our time more effectively," I added.

Noticing that Al had been uncharacteristically quiet, I asked him if he had anything to add.

"For me it just seemed like a waste of time."

"What actually happened for you during the experiment?"

"I sat there thinking, 'What are we doing this for? When is it going to be over?'"

"So Al, what does it tell you about Brenda that she almost fell asleep and wanted to keep sleeping?"

"That she's exhausted and needs a break."

"How about Christi?"

"She pushes so hard in one direction that it's hard for her to shift gears."

"And how about someone who refuses to play at all?" I asked him. "What conclusion would you draw about that person?"

His eyes narrowed and he drew his mouth into a tight-lipped smile.

"This team needs you, Al," I continued. "But you're not going to be much use to them or yourself playing with a full cup."

He started to laugh.

"I see what you mean," he finally said. "I guess it's easier to see how other people are screwing up than it is to see that about yourself."

"Often the things we like least about other people's behavior are the things we need to work on ourselves," I said. "That's what your team needs to know–are you willing to work on yourself in the interest of helping them succeed?"

"Meaning what exactly?"

"Why don't we ask your teammates?" I suggested.

"If you would just consider what's right about something before you tell me everything you think is wrong with it, that would be a huge relief," said Brenda. "I feel like we get stuck arguing right and wrong instead of evaluating costs and benefits."

"I disagree, totally!" Al said, and then he broke the uncomfortable tension with a sly grin. "I'm only kidding. Maybe I've been taking the easy way out. It's easier to poke holes in something than it is to take a risk. But I guess the time has come. If we try something and it doesn't work out, what's the worst they can do? Fire us?"

That was worth a laugh from the rest of the team.

What We See Depends on Where We Stand

"Brenda, I'd like to return to the distinction you made between right/wrong thinking versus cost/benefit. Confusion between these two approaches can create huge pacing problems." I said. "For example, the question of unrealistic deadlines often becomes a right/wrong debate. Isn't that what you described happening between you and Tom, Christi? "

"You bet. If only he would recognize that we've got to get past this power struggle and look at the possibility that we might have to make some hard trade-offs."

"That's interesting," said Brenda, "because when you and I have this conversation, I face the same problem with you."

"When Christi communicates with Tom, she's downstream talking up," I said. "When she talks with you Brenda, the roles get reversed. As we switch positions in the system, we often find our point of view shifting as well. Remember that Al adopted many of the behaviors he most objects to in senior management the minute he sat in the A chair," I added.

"Hey, don't go sticking me in the middle of their dispute. My cup is full already," Al teased.

"Christi, why do you think the conflict between you and Tom gets repeated when you deal with Brenda?" I asked.

"The truth is, when I hear complaints about inadequate time, I'm afraid it's a way of hiding poor planning, inadequate communication, and sloppy implementation," she admitted.

"Do you think those are the fears Tom has when he hears you raise questions about expanding scope?" I asked her.

She paused. "I wouldn't be surprised."

Respecting Limits

"How we think about deadlines depends on whether we believe we've reached our limit," said Ellen.

"What do you mean?" I asked her.

"Once we've hit our limits, we're forced to make hard trade-offs. If half the people are pulled from a project, either that project will take twice as long to finish, or the scope will have to be significantly reduced in order to hit the original deadline. On the other hand, if management can squeeze more capacity out of the remaining folks, maybe nothing will have to be sacrificed."

"Actually *we* get sacrificed," objected Dave. "We work more days and longer hours without compensation. The cost just gets shifted to us."

"That's why that conversation so easily becomes a power struggle," Ellen added.

"It's also the wrong conversation to have before any real detailed planning has been done," said Christi. "Like we said earlier, we need to suspend judgment on what's possible until we actually run the numbers. Maybe we can actually find ways to increase our efficiency without increasing our workload."

"Since we won't collect that data until later in the planning process, we'll defer the conversation about whether or not we've reached our limit until later. But we can begin to think about trade-offs now. At some point every project pushes up against some limiting factor. What trade-offs will best serve the project and the customer when that moment comes? That's the kind of question we want to begin asking," I suggested.

"Why fix something that ain't broke?" said Al. "Wouldn't it be more efficient to wait until the problem occurs and then address it?"

"Have you ever played a game that bogged down in a dispute over the rules?" I asked him. "You'll notice it usually happens at a crucial point. When someone hits a line drive right down the foul line that scores the go-ahead run in the bottom of the ninth, you don't want to start debating where the foul line is. If one team claims it was marked by the shirt while the other team insists that it was the tree stump, you've got a serious problem that's going to leave one side or the other very unhappy. Before that game starts, nobody really cares whether it's the stump or the shirt. You just want the decision to be clear. But once victory hangs in the balance, it's going to be a very long and unpleasant argument. That's why effective pacing is so important. If we can address key questions before stuff hits the fan, we will make better decisions in less time."

I also pointed out to them that different people would make different assumptions as to what action to take when a limit is hit. For example, if we lose a month out of our schedule, can I assume that we will simply deliver the project one month later than originally planned? If not, will I be given additional resources to make up for lost time, or should I reduce the scope? If these decisions have not been made explicit before the crisis hits, people can begin adjusting in different directions. This creates many of the predictable project breakdowns we saw reproduced in the Project Game.

The Trade-off Matrix—Weigh Options

The Trade-off Matrix provides a graphic tool for getting these assumptions on the table and sorting them out. Project limits are measured in three dimensions: scope (what you will deliver), time (when you will deliver it), and resources (how much it will cost). Whenever we alter one dimension, the others tend to shift as well.

In Ellen's example, a reduction in resources (the number of people working on her project) means that she will either need more time to accomplish the same amount of work, or else she will have to reduce the number of features and overall quality if the same deadline must be hit.

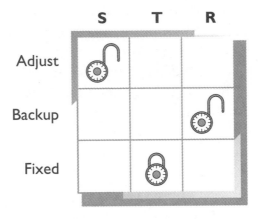

A decision to reduce the scope (S) of the project to accommodate an immovable deadline (T) could be graphically illustrated as shown above

The locks can be moved to indicate which of these parameters is "set in stone," which one we would adjust first to deal with an unexpected crisis, and which we would resort to only as a backup strategy.

To understand the backup strategy, consider the following situation. To have a product ready to demonstrate at a trade show, scope has been reduced to its bare minimum. However, even this bare–bones version of the product is running late and will probably require an extra day or two beyond the available time to be fully functional. We cannot reduce scope any further, but perhaps we can recruit some additional help to get us out the door by the required deadline. Reducing scope was the first thing we did to try and hit the deadline. When that could not be reduced further, some small increase in resources became our fallback position to deliver the project on time.

"I like the idea of the matrix," said Christi. "I think we often talk about these potential risks, but this approach formalizes the process and clears up any miscommunication."

"I agree," said Brenda. "I also like how it gets us past the debate about where the limit line is and instead focuses our attention on what our options are once we're there."

"I think it's a good tool," said Dave, "but it takes time. When we're already running behind schedule, I just don't see us doing this."

"You're right, Dave," I said. "The warp speed world runs on a need for speed: faster chips, faster routers, faster networks, faster decision making, and, above all, faster time to market. If you snooze, you lose! Here's the catch. In order to run that fast, you have to run on automatic. If you need to stop and think about what you're doing, it slows you down. But many of those automatic settings do not produce the results you want. That's what tripped you up in the Project Game."

Slow Down to Turn

Effective pacing means that, at certain points, we're going to trade speed for accuracy. Think of it this way: you're racing to a friend's house at sixty miles per hour. You come to a stretch of road on which you know you'll have to make a turn, but you can't remember exactly which street to turn on. If you want to read the street signs to find the right road, you're going to slow down. If you miss the turn, the speed is useless.

You'll probably brake going into the turn as well. In other words, when you're making key connections or changing direction, it pays to slow down. When you know the turf or have a wide-open stretch of road, you can open it up. Involving people takes time. Is it worth it? What's the cost if we do? Just as important, what's the cost if we don't? In other words, what are the pros and cons of inclusion, which happens to be rule number 3? But before moving on to the third rule, I wanted to summarize the guidelines we had just discussed.

The following reminders distilled the essence of our inquiry:

PACING GUIDELINES

- Stop periodically and

empty your cup.

- Respect limits;

weigh options.

- Slow down to turn.

7

······

Avoid Confusion through Inclusion

We had already tackled many of the challenges on the Warp Speed Barrier Checklist. The Trade-off Matrix provided a way to weigh options in the face of unrealistic deadlines. Reciprocal relationship helped us translate values into motivation and resolve conflict. Managing "unrealistic" deadlines required recognizing that we're all in this together and that there is always a way through. With this attitude and the right information, we can find a way to work through the changes. All of this adds up to improved communication.

But the pressure of warp speed to keep us running on automatic makes it difficult to translate these new behaviors into action. That's why it's essential to keep the new approaches simple and easy to apply to everyday challenges. This is particularly important when it comes to inclusion, because it does take extra time to make it happen. Is it worth it? Once again, we began with a simple experiment.

"Imagine throwing your suitcases in the trunk of the car and setting off with your loved ones on a long-awaited vacation," I said. "After driving for a couple of hours, you look over at your partner and say, 'So, where do you think we should go?' That's not the best time to be making that decision. If you packed nothing but swim suits and snorkeling gear, hopefully the family doesn't decide on Alaska! Including people in the decision after its been made and acted upon doesn't make much sense.

"Nonetheless, the warp speed world tries to run projects using this approach on a daily basis. As we saw in the Project Game, this practice is often justified with the excuse that telling everyone the goal would take too long. What would you say to someone making this case?" I asked the group.

"I would point out that they are only considering the additional time required up front but are neglecting the enormous inefficiencies that result when key contributors are running blind," said Brenda.

"I think the time required for effectively communicating the goal is also overestimated because we have never really learned to do it right," Ellen added.

"Well, we can begin to correct that problem immediately," I said.

So saying, I handed each of them a small slip of paper and asked them to read it as quickly as possible. The message on the paper read:

FINISHED FILES ARE THE RE-
SULT OF YEARS OF SCIENTIF-
IC STUDY COMBINED WITH
THE EXPERIENCE OF MANY
YEARS OF EXPERTS.

When they were done, I then asked them to imagine the room we were in as a huge clock face with twelve o'clock at the front of the room, three o'clock over by the windows, six o'clock at the rear, and nine o'clock off to my right by the whiteboards. With this in mind, they were instructed to reread their slips of paper, count the number of letter *F*s, and move to that position on the clock.

Al, Christi, and Dave counted three *F*s and found themselves clustered together by the windows. With five, Brenda found herself toward the back of the room. A few feet to her right stood Ellen. She counted seven. Since they didn't know that the message on each of their slips of paper was exactly the same, the oddness of this situation was not immediately apparent.

I took Ellen's slip of paper with seven *F*s and gave it to Dave, returning Dave's three *F*s to Ellen. When asked, once again, to count the letter *F*s, both of them still found the same number they had before.

"Do you understand that he said *F*, not *S*?" Al called across the room to Ellen.

"Maybe it's because English is her second language," Dave whispered to Al. Since they were in the majority, it was hard to imagine that the problem stemmed from something they were missing.

"All of your messages are the same," I told them. "Look at the word 'of' and you should count seven *F*s."

Christi laughed, Al muttered something uncomplimentary about his own intelligence, and Dave, sounding like a country store clerk watching a traveling medicine show, exclaimed, "I'll be!"

Increase Feedback to Catch the Missing *F*s

"There are a number of explanations as to why this happens," I told the team. "For our purposes, it is useful to recognize that our brains have evolved a sophisticated series of filters to handle the extraordinary complexity of life. These filters quickly determine which stimuli are important and make them foreground and which are unimportant and can be relegated to the background. Once we decide something is background, it becomes virtually invisible. 'That's what happened to the word *of*. It got filtered out."

"That's pretty scary," said Brenda. "If we're missing that much detail in a little five–line message, I hate to think what's falling through the cracks in the warp speed complexity of our projects."

"A big part of the problem stemmed from our physical separation," Christi observed. "Since the clock–face setup kept Ellen physically distant from those of us who only saw three *Fs*, there was no opportunity to compare notes."

"That's why an inclusive team process is so important at each stage of project planning," I added. To help them better visualize the specific points at which this feedback becomes necessary, I showed them the following diagram:

Inclusive Planning

"The first step in our planning process, once we've clearly defined our goal, is to decide on all the tasks needed to accomplish that goal."

"You mean we need to create a 'To Do' list," said Brenda, referring to the diagram.

"That's right, and in project jargon we call that 'To Do' list a work breakdown structure, or WBS. The important thing to remember here is that this is a team process and should not be done by the project manager alone. Is that how you're doing it currently?" I asked Brenda.

"Pretty much," she said. "Generally I have team members submit a list defining how long they think each of their tasks will take. Then I compile that information into a master list and ask for feedback."

"I recognize that, at times, that approach is necessary because of the nature of distributed teams," I said. "However, when the team is unable to meet face-to-face, you break the immediacy of feedback and increase the likelihood of missing *Fs* dramatically. Also, if you have no choice but to work in this fashion, it becomes all the more important that you have established a face-to-face relationship previously. The more anonymous you are to each other, the harder it is to get solid commitments and the more likely you will fall victim to the miscommunication we saw in the Project Game."

"Don't I know it!" said Brenda emphatically.

"So once we have a task list, what comes next?" I asked the group.

"We need to sequence them," said Al. "We need to see how all the pieces fit together into one big picture."

"Exactly. We now want to look at the task list and ask ourselves, 'What depends on what?' That's why this big picture of linked tasks is called a dependency diagram."

"Is that the same thing as PERT or CPM?" Ellen wanted to know.

"That's right," I said.

"And the zigzagging line in your diagram illustrates that at each level of planning we clarify more and more of our assumptions, capture increasing levels of missed detail, and so draw an increasingly tighter bead on the target?" Christi asked somewhat rhetorically.

"Yes, that's why bringing the entire core team together is so important. It's through this ongoing feedback that we progressively refine our understanding."

"What's 'optimization'?" asked Dave.

I explained to him that the first pass at creating the dependency diagram produces a somewhat ideal picture. Just as an artist does a sketch and then adds the base colors before brushing in the fine detail, you will build your project plan in layers. The dependency diagram is like your base coat–it shows how the tasks will be sequenced. However, this sequencing may present an idealized picture, which may not accurately reflect some real-world problems. For example, the diagram might indicate that you will miss your desired deadline or that you have overscheduled a key contributor. Optimization adjusts the diagram to handle those limitations. If the diagram suggests that you will run longer than your original estimate, you could increase the number of parallel tasks, remove excessive padding, or eliminate some tasks to reduce scope.

Risk analysis and contingency planning perform much the same function by taking into account problems that might derail the project in the future.

"It still seems to me that we can spend all this time talking and planning for nothing," said Al. "The way we change priorities in this company, plans aren't worth the paper they're written on."

"That's the whole point of effective planning," Christi said with a hint of exasperation in her voice. "It enables us to map detours around the unexpected."

How You Plan Is How You Play

"Al's not the only one who's going to raise objections to additional planning sessions," said Brenda. "People resist change, and they already complain about being over-loaded with meetings. Couldn't we accomplish the same thing using e-mail?"

"All we had to do to break the feedback loop was separate you by a few feet," I reminded her. "Without the benefit of immediate, person-to-person feedback, it becomes much harder to catch the missing *Fs*. Keep in mind that we are doing a lot more than collecting information. We are also practicing how we will work together as a team–How you plan is how you play. E-mail increases speed but reduces quality, and that can set a pattern for the rest of your project."

"If the customer contact has gotten proper specifications, I don't know what we need to get together and talk about," Al objected. "I agree with Brenda. It's a lot easier and faster to send everyone the spec electronically."

"If numerical specifications were all we needed to define the goal effectively, I would agree with you, but they're not. Confusion over this point dooms many projects before they've gotten off the ground. Customers want solutions, not specifications, and they expect us to deliver the goods."

Solutions versus Specifications

Upon further discussion, we agreed that a spec tells you what to do but not necessarily why it matters. As the Project Game demonstrated, clearly defined tasks without a context can generate all kinds of miscues and inefficiencies. A well-defined goal demands that we get to know our customer's hopes and fears. The goal-setting process should enable us to answer questions like these:

- How will our work be used, under what conditions?
- What result does the customer hope to achieve?
- Do we understand the customer's prioritization of features and benefits?

"In other words, goal setting is as much about building relationships with our customers as it is about getting the numbers right. This is a key inclusion step that gets overlooked by teams rushing toward implementation," I cautioned them.

"But we don't have direct access to our customer in most cases," Dave objected.

"All the more reason why you need to maintain an excellent relationship with those who do. If marketing provides your customer contact, defining them as the 'idiots out there' gets in the way of clearly understanding the solution from the customer's point of view. Sometimes people focus solely on specifications because they are uncomfortable with the imprecision of interpersonal communication. They neglect the fact that we can deliver a project that fulfills the written specification in every detail but still leave the customer unhappy. Have any of you had this experience?" I asked.

Customers Want Solutions

Al raised his hand.

"The last company I worked for produced industrial components. We won a large contract building specialized fluorescent ballasts for one of our major clients.

"Prior to starting the project, the engineering group spent a lot of time with the customer going over all the numbers making sure we understood the specifications perfectly. The finished products we built fulfilled the specifications in every detail, but the client was extremely unhappy because the fixtures generated a low-level buzz. The client refused to pay the invoice because of this. It was a real nightmare. In all the technical conferences, the issue of noise had never come up and so was never factored into the specifications."

"Thanks, Al," I said. "That's a perfect example of a very widespread breakdown. Clients expect us to provide much more than flawless technical expertise; they want solutions. They rely on our knowledge and experience to guide them through unfamiliar territory and to point out subtle factors (like ballast noise) that they may not know they don't know. Nailing the technical specifications is not enough. If we have an unhappy customer, we have an unsuccessful project."

Reviewing who needs to be included, we identified these key points: The project manager must clarify with the customer contact or project owner exactly what solution is required. He or she should then include the core team in developing a complete understanding of that goal and create a Trade-off Matrix. The goal and matrix should be reviewed and signed off by the project owner. The core team should be included in developing the To Do list (WBS) and dependency diagram. They should also participate in reworking or optimizing this plan and considering contingency plans. The completed project plan should be reviewed by the project owner and approved.

In other words, we emphasize inclusion as a way to increase both feedback and input. No one person can think of, much less monitor, all of the many variables that impact project success.

1. In the F exercise, we demonstrated how easily different people can examine the exact same information but see very different things. Without the ability to catch and reconcile these differences, projects are in trouble.

2. It's also easy to become so preoccupied with detail that we lose sight of the forest for the trees. Consequently, when we think about inclusion, we want to make sure to include the customer and not just the members of our team.

3. Customers want solutions, which our technically perfect products may fail to satisfy unless we've continued to check back with them continuously throughout the process.

4. Of course, increased inclusion demands more time up front. Think about how much time gets wasted redoing and undoing mistakes and you will find that it is time well spent. If you neglect communication and inclusion during the planning of your project, why would you expect it to appear suddenly when you attempt to execute the project?

5. Planning is not just time you spend getting ready to do something. How you plan is how you play.

6. Increased inclusion provides the most reliable protection against every complaint on the Warp Speed Barrier Checklist. The payoff is an enhanced level of fulfillment for both the people and the project.

INCLUSION GUIDELINES

- **Increase feedback to catch the missing *F*s.**

- **Customers define solutions so keep in touch.**

- **How you plan is how you play.**

8

Fulfill Both People and Project

What does it mean to be fulfilled? Is delivering a project to specification, on time, and within budget an adequate definition? It's not if our customer is unhappy. And what does it mean for each of us to be fulfilled in the midst of our overscheduled, warp speed, multitasking? Increasing our levels of power and speed may be the right criterion when shopping for a new computer, but is it really the standard by which we want to measure our lives? When was the last time we stopped and asked ourselves, "Where are we rushing to?"

When people must flee their homes in the face of an impending disaster, what do they take? What would we take? Maybe we'd grab the family photo album or some precious keepsake that could not be replaced. In the final analysis, what we really value is the love. How many times have we reminded one another that no one lying on his deathbed has ever said, "Gee, I wish I had spent more time at the office"? Why? There's not enough love.

Yet, all the things that we have identified as essential for project success—effective communication, making and keeping commitments, harmonizing layers of the system, reciprocal relationships–lead us in this direction. They point toward greater caring, trust, respect, and openness–in other words, toward love.

As you might imagine, talking about love in the context of project management was a bit much for Al. I tried to reassure him by explaining that this all had a very practical application. The quickest way to see how effectively a team was exercising all that we had talked about was to attend one of their meetings. Meetings provide a good indication as to how they work together and also tend to accurately reflect the larger company culture. Consequently, if you can change your meetings, you can begin to change your culture.

I began by asking them what they thought about their meetings.

Meeting Barriers

"That's an easy enough question to answer," said Al. "For the most part our meetings are unfocused time wasters."

Brenda responded immediately. There was a hint of defensiveness in her voice. "With the number of strong personalities we have to contend with," she said, shooting a pointed glance in Al's direction, "keeping meetings focused can sometimes be a challenge. We do the best we can given the circumstances. Sure meetings can be frustrating, but they are necessary. Sometimes they just take too long."

"Ellen, Dave, anything you'd like to add?" I asked.

"It depends on the meeting," Ellen said. "Some of the meetings I attend are very efficient and productive, while others keep revisiting the same issues over and over while never really producing any action items."

"I agree with everything that's been said already," said Dave, "but I'd also like to add my frustration with people constantly coming late and leaving early. In many of the meetings I attend, the same few people dominate the discussions and resort to personal attacks when they disagree."

"So let's see what we've got," I said. "Your list of meeting complaints include they're unfocused and take too long, you revisit the same issues and fail to produce action items, people come late and leave early, the same few people dominate, and some participants resort to personal attacks. Those are pretty standard complaints. Any ideas as to what we can do about them?"

Agenda Fundamentals

"Well," said Ellen, "one obvious solution for meetings that are unfocused, take too long, and keep revisiting the same issues is stick to the agenda."

"That assumes that we have an agenda to begin with," Al added.

"It also helps to distribute an agenda at least twenty-four hours in advance of the meeting so that people can come prepared," I suggested. "This, of course, rarely happens and is another glaring example of failing to do what we already know. Why do you think something so obviously useful, like an agenda, gets so consistently neglected?"

"We're just too busy," said Brenda. "We start fighting fires and juggling priorities the minute we walk out of one meeting and don't have a chance to catch our breath until the next one rolls around."

"Sounds like we've got a pacing problem," said Christi.

"Try reserving the last few minutes of your meetings to draft a preliminary agenda for the next one," I suggested. "This takes it off your To Do list and helps address the problem of being too busy. It also allows the entire team to participate, which reinforces your commitment to broader inclusion. Finally, it ensures that everyone has a copy of the agenda in advance of your next meeting so they can come better prepared."

"But even with an agenda, how do you keep the meeting from running too long?" asked Brenda.

"Do you specify times for each item when you create an agenda?" I asked her in return.

"No, most of the time I don't."

"Again, it's a simple thing but it usually does the trick. Everyone wants to get done on time and back to work as quickly as possible; time marks help the entire team meet that objective."

"But what can we do about people who just love to hear themselves talk?" Dave asked with some exasperation.

"And let's not forget the personal attacks," Brenda added.

Using Ground Rules

"While the agenda helps focus the content side of the meeting, drafting a set of ground rules makes it a lot easier to manage the interpersonal challenges–particularly when you find yourself dealing with difficult people," I told them.

"Ground rules provide a set of agreed–to guidelines that enable meetings to run smoothly and effectively. They include agreements such as

- start on time;
- stick to the agenda;
- no personal attacks, and so forth.

"In fact, they are so obvious," I continued, "it almost seems like either an insult or a waste of time to bring them up at all. Don't believe it! They may be elementary, but they are also consistently violated, and their neglect causes most of the frustrations that plague meetings."

"That's all we need is a bunch of new rules," said Al sarcastically, "and what is somebody going to do to me if I break one of them?"

"Do you play any sports, Al?" I asked him.

He seemed to register a certain surprise at the apparent incongruity of my question but responded, nonetheless, by saying that he participated in a company softball league.

"Do you have a set of rules you play by?"

"Of course we do," he almost scoffed. "If you don't have rules, you can't play the game."

"Exactly my point. We're all just trying to play a game we call 'business' where we all hope to have some fun and make some money. People can't play by the rules if they don't know what they are. As we saw in the Project Game, when people are forced to guess at the rules, they wind up playing at cross-purposes. Meeting ground rules are not something anybody is going to impose on you. You will make them up yourselves so that you can all commit to playing the same game. Does this make a little more sense?"

"Yeah, I see your point. But how is that going to eliminate the time I waste listening to people go on and on about issues that don't concern me?"

"Having an agenda and sticking to the agreed-on time marks should deal with that," said Brenda.

Separate Status from Problem Solving

"That should help a lot," I agreed. "Another important way to cut down on wasted time in meetings is to separate status review from problem solving. When a task owner fails to meet a planned completion date, a small subset of the meeting frequently dives into overly detailed technical discussions that hold little relevance or interest for the rest of the meeting participants."

"That's it exactly," said Al. "And I see what you're attempting to do with this approach. Not having to sit through technical brainstorming sessions that have nothing to do with me would be great, but it also sounds like having to attend both status review meetings and separate problem-solving sessions is just going to increase my total number of meetings. That's the last thing I'm looking for."

"I understand your concern. You do not need to call additional meetings to tackle the problem solving," I reassured him. "Just hold off on them until after the status review is complete. At that point, anyone who does not need to participate in the problem-solving session can get back to work."

I explained that when a variance occurred, they should allow no more than five minutes for discussion about possible fixes within the status review meeting. If more time was needed, the people involved should continue their problem solving in the second portion of the meeting. By adhering to this simple practice, the length of many status review meetings could be cut in half. Then, by continuing with the problem-solving session immediately, you ensure that key action items are being addressed.

The Importance of Action Items

"I'm glad you mentioned action items," said Christi. "The failure to complete action items confirms the widely held belief that meetings waste time. Why meet if nothing actually gets done? On the other hand, when people see that, week after week, the time and energy they invest in meeting pays off in meaningful change, their commitment level increases significantly."

"Thanks, Christi. Getting people to take accountability for action items is, in one sense, the underpinning of your entire project culture," I said. "If you can't trust people to do what they say, you can't manage your project. Your meetings provide a practice field for refining this fundamental skill of making and keeping commitments."

"If we implemented the few things we've just talked about, our meetings would improve a thousand percent," said Dave. "My concern is that we walk out of here and everything slips back to business as usual. What can we do to make sure we actually do this stuff?"

Evaluating Success

"Try this quick end-of-meeting evaluation technique. At the end of each meeting, prepare a flip chart or whiteboard with a plus (+) column and a minus (–) column. Begin by asking people what they liked about the meeting, and record that in the plus column. Next, ask people what could go better next time and capture that in the minus column.

"The first time you try this, people may feel reluctant to criticize and so will offer humorous critiques that sound silly or trivial. For example, they might suggest that you have bagels as well as donuts. Whatever they say, just write it down," I suggested. "Imagine their reaction when they walk into the next meeting and find bagels on the table. What message does that send?"

"They see that they've been heard," said Dave.

"They also see that what they had to say actually made a difference," Ellen added.

"Yes, and for many people that is a startling experience," I agreed. "The more opportunities you can create for people to experience that they matter, that they are listened to, and that their contributions make a difference, the stronger your team becomes. This three-minute exercise provides an easy way to create that experience. It also leads to better meetings."

"It seems to me," began Ellen, "that these five simple steps–agenda, ground rules, separate status review from problem solving, enforce action items, and conduct an end-of-meeting evaluation–reinforce the four fundamentals we've been discussing all day long."

Change Your Meetings, Change Your Culture

"I would take it even a step further," I added. "Meetings are a microcosm of a company's culture. Change the meetings, and the culture starts to change as well. That's the bigger payoff that can result from making these relatively minor adjustments."

"I agree with all of that," said Brenda, "but don't we run the risk of seeming manipulative, trying all these new techniques?"

"You could," I acknowledged. "It all depends on your intention. If you're using these techniques so that you can have greater control, then you will probably be accused of being manipulative. If, on the other hand, your goal is to increase inclusion, invite commitment, and create greater opportunities for fulfillment, that's probably what people will perceive. What people get are your true intentions. Besides, manipulative behavior tends to be a big waste of time and energy since we rarely succeed in changing other people's behavior. We will experience much greater success and satisfaction by making sure that we do the right thing and let go of outcome."

Every project, every meeting, and every task we involve ourselves in presents us with a series of choices. Will our fight–or–flight–programming run us, or will we work from the zone? Do we run the whole race pedal to the metal or pace ourselves so that we can make the key connections and necessary turns? Can we resist our desire for control long enough to include others, so they can help us catch the missing *Fs*? And will we love ourselves and others enough to insist that both the people and the project be fulfilled?

These are the choices that frame a successful career and a meaningful life. Projects, by providing clear and immediate feedback to our actions, keep prodding us to become the people we really want to be.

FULFILLMENT GUIDELINES

- Change your meetings, change your culture.

- If you don't have rules, you can't play the game.

- What people get are your true intentions.

9

Words into Action

Tom and Christi delivered the results that satisfied corporate. Consequently, I got to continue working with teams throughout their division for several years. But for me, the most satisfying payoff was a note that I received from Ellen about a year after that initial session. Here's what she said:

Hi, Barry,

Sorry it's taken so long for me to send you this e-mail like I promised.

Soon after our training session Christi promoted me to project manager, and the challenges of my new position have changed my life—for the better. I want to thank you for the contribution you made in helping me get here.

After formally taking on the role as project manager, I had my first opportunity to try the techniques a few months later on a systems integration project. There was much resistance to the project initially. Also, 15–25 people attended our early planning meetings physically and by phone conference, and that was a mistake. As a result, there was a lot of conflict, and it took three hours to get the information I needed in order to do the initial plan. I've now learned that effective inclusion during a planning session requires keeping the numbers down to ten or less.

After this meeting, I used the F exercise as a reference point to break through some of the resistance. I also asked Christi to attend a team meeting so everyone could vent to her directly, and she was able to help me establish the necessary level of credibility and authority I needed. This enabled all of us to start working from the zone by clearing some of the conflict. But the real breakthrough came when I went to Dallas, TX, to meet the rest of my team face-to-face.

Initially, given the enormous time pressure I face to complete this project, I felt very reluctant to spend the time to make this trip. Then I remembered everything we had said about the importance of pacing and inclusion. With that in mind, I just went ahead and booked the flight. The results were amazing.

I felt some of the most reluctant team members relax a bit once we got to know each other and go to lunch. Some of us even went out to a local bar after work to let off some steam. Our team's relationship has improved significantly since that trip. I am going to make another trip to Dallas in the next few months to continue this success. I now realize that effective inclusion can have as much to do with what we do outside the office as it does with how we run our meetings.

Since this first difficult experience, our team has received great praise from our executive staff for the project plan we presented. I have reduced my core team down to ten people in order to optimize our final plan using your techniques. Because of this, we were able to cut down the process to about an hour and a half.

Also, it was very useful to attend your class again on 3/13 with my core team to continue to the next phase of our project. Most of my team now understands what I am trying to do in order to plan our projects. We now have a common language and common experience. My team no longer feels like I am putting them through Hell. To make it easier for the folks who have not yet been through the training, I put together a one-page summary of the rules, which has definitely helped. I've enclosed a copy. Let me know what you think

Finally, I owe much of my current success to the deeper understanding I now have of my job and our project team. That would not have been possible without the Rules of Warp Speed.

Thanks again, for all your help.
Ellen

I've always loved how clearly Ellen spells out the trial-and-error process she went through. First she tried including the entire team and found that twenty-five people were too many, so she pared it down to ten. When she met with initial resistance, she tried some of the exercises we learned in class, but she also called on Christi to help her establish credibility. Her instincts told her to fly to Dallas and meet with the rest of her team. When the "not-enough-time demon" tried to dissuade her, she used the pacing guidelines to keep on track. Her insight that "effective inclusion can have as much to do with what we do outside the office as it does with how we run our meetings" is so important, and it bears repeating.

In other words, Ellen demonstrates how to apply these guidelines in the real world. They act more as a compass than as a map. Use them to keep you pointed in the right direction, and trust your instincts to reveal the path.

The Warp Speed
Game Plan

Project success depends on our ability to make and keep clear commitments. This requires a shift from power–based to reciprocal relationships and ongoing attention to effective communication. These fundamentals are captured in the rule that reminds us to:

Avoid Confusion through Inclusion

1. Increase feedback to catch the missing *Fs*.
2. Since customers define solutions, keep in touch.
3. How you plan Is how you play.

Inclusion breaks down under pressure. That pressure may stem from inner fears or our tendency to do too much and move too quickly The next two rules provide guidelines for managing these issues.

When confronting fear remember:

Work from the Zone

1. We're in this together.
2. There's always a way through.
3. See where you really are.

When running on overload try to:

Shift from Racing to Pacing

1. Periodically empty your cup.
2. Respect limits; weigh options.
3. Slow down to turn.

Commited, satisfied project contributors are more likely to produce happy satisfied customers. That's why the fourth rule reminds us that:

Both the Project and the People Must Be Fulfilled

1. Change your meetings, change your culture.
2. It you don't have rules, you can't play the game.
3. What people get are your true intentions.

Every time you think this will take too much time, remember how much time it takes to screw up and be miserable. It's your choice–why not go for it?

Index

About the Author

Barry Flicker is founder of Basic Training, a company based in the San Francisco Bay area that offers a complete curriculum of courses in management and professional development to organizations intent on keeping pace with the rapid transformations of the global economy.

He has authored texts for courses on project management, collaborative negotiating, conflict resolution, nonlinear problem solving, meeting management, and effective communication. His work helps free people from the limiting assumptions and counterproductive behavior blocking their success. The immediate applicability of this approach has made him one of the most sought-after experts in Silicon Valley and throughout the country.

In addition to a "Who's Who" list of corporate clients, Flicker's work has, for years, been utilized as part of the professional development curriculum of the Institute of Electrical and Electronics Engineers (IEEE). His Project Game has become part of one of the leading business incubation courses in the country taught at the University of California–Berkeley.

Flicker's success as a trainer, consultant, writer, and speaker reflect a colorful personal history that has included touring with a rock band, performing as a stage magician, working the comedy clubs of San Francisco, and serving as a whitewater river guide. He and his wife live in Marin County, California, with their fish Roshi and a constant flow of kids.

Working with the
Author

Barry Flicker Basic Training

The Master Class in project management is supported by a
complete curriculum, which includes training and coach-
ing expertise in communications, negotiating, conflict resolution, nonlinear problem solving, meeting management,
team building, and leadership. Intact project teams, project
managers, program managers, individual contributors, as
well as anyone frustrated by getting a group of people to
deliver by a deadline, will come away from this work
ready to tap a new capacity for satisfaction and effectiveness.

> Barry Flicker & Basic Training
> P.O. Box 194
> Woodacre, CA 94973
> Office: (415) 488–0805; fax: (415) 488–0571;
> e–mail: bflk@attbi.com
> Web site: www.barryflicker.com

Berrett-Koehler Publishers

BERRETT-KOEHLER is an independent publisher of books, periodicals, and other publications at the leading edge of new thinking and innovative practice on work, business, management, leadership, stewardship, career development, human resources, entrepreneurship, and global sustainability.

Since the company's founding in 1992, we have been committed to supporting the movement toward a more enlightened world of work by publishing books, periodicals, and other publications that help us to integrate our values with our work and work lives, and to create more humane and effective organizations.

We have chosen to focus on the areas of work, business, and organizations, because these are central elements in many people's lives today. Furthermore, the work world is going through tumultuous changes, from the decline of job security to the rise of new structures for organizing people and work. We believe that change is needed at all levels—individual, organizational, community, and global—and our publications address each of these levels.

We seek to create new lenses for understanding organizations, to legitimize topics that people care deeply about but that current business orthodoxy censors or considers secondary to bottom-line concerns, and to uncover new meaning, means, and ends for our work and work lives.

See next pages for other publications from Berrett-Koehler

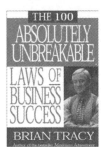

How to Get Ideas

Jack Foster
Illustrated by Larry Corby

In *How to Get Ideas,* Jack Foster draws on three decades of experience as an advertising writer and creative director to take the mystery and anxiety out of getting ideas. Describing eight ways to condition your mind to produce ideas and five subsequent steps for creating and implementing ideas on command, he makes it easy, fun, and understandable.

Paperback, 150 pages • ISBN 1-57675-006-X
Item #5006X-397 $14.95

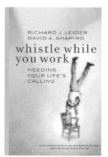

Whistle While You Work
Heeding Your Life's Calling

Richard J. Leider and David A. Shapiro

We all have have a calling in life. It needs only to be uncovered, not discovered. *Whistle While You Work* makes the uncovering process inspiring and fun. Featuring a unique "Calling Card" exercise—a powerful way to put the whistle in your work—it is a liberating and practical guide that will help you find work that is truly satisfying, deeply fulfilling, and consistent with your deepest values.

Paperback original, 200 pages • ISBN 1-57675-103-1
Item #51031-397 $15.95

Repacking Your Bags
Lighten Your Load for the Rest of Your Life

Richard J. Leider and David A. Shapiro

Learn how to climb out from under the many burdens you're carrying and find the fulfillment that's missing in your life. A simple yet elegant process teaches you to balance the demands of work, love, and place in order to create and live your own vision of success.

Paperback, 234 pages, 2/96 • ISBN 1-881052-87-7
Item #52877-397 $14.95

Hardcover, 1/95 • ISBN 1-881052-67-2 • Item no. 52672-397 $21.95

Audio, 2 cassettes • ISBN 1-57453-027-5 • Item #30275-397 $17.95

Berrett-Koehler Publishers
PO Box 565, Williston, VT 05495-9900
Call toll-free! **800-929-2929** 7 am-12 midnight

Or fax your order to 802-864-7627
For fastest service order online: **www.bkconnection.com**